BEAUTIFULLY WRECKED
Lives Altered by an Unexpected Collision

Published in Beaverton, Oregon, by Good Catch Publishing.
www.goodcatchpublishing.com
V1.1

Printed in the United States of America

TABLE OF CONTENTS

DEDICATION

This book is dedicated to Ted Brinkman, a hero to many.
His life was beautifully wrecked in 1956 at the age of 27.
It was because of that unexpected collision that he began
to live life with the same passion and drive as he did
before, only for a different cause.
It is because of Ted's life, courage, love and passion
that these stories are being told in this book today.

Thank you, Dad, for being the man you were and living
life the way you did.
I love you and thank you for what you have passed on
to me as well as so many others.

Ted Brinkman, August 26, 1929 - June 22, 2009

Love,
Ben Brinkman

ACKNOWLEDGEMENTS

I would like to thank Ben Brinkman for his vision for this book and Tranica Esperas for her hard work in making it a reality. And to the people of Canvas, thank you for your boldness and vulnerability in sharing your personal stories.

This book would not have been published without the amazing efforts of our project manager and editor, Marla Lindstrom Benroth. Her untiring resolve pushed this project forward and turned it into a stunning victory. Thank you for your great fortitude and diligence. Deep thanks to our incredible Editor in Chief, Michelle Cuthrell, and Executive Editor, Nicole Phinney Lowell, for all the amazing work they do. I would also like to thank our invaluable proofreader, Melody Davis, for the focus and energy she has put into perfecting our words.

Lastly, I want to extend our gratitude to the creative and very talented Ann Clayton, who designed the beautiful cover for *Beautifully Wrecked: Lives Altered by an Unexpected Collision.*

Daren Lindley
President and CEO
Good Catch Publishing

The book you are about to read
is a compilation of authentic life stories.
The facts are true, and the events are real.
These storytellers have dealt with crisis, tragedy, abuse
and neglect and have shared their most private moments,
mess-ups and hang-ups in order for others to learn and
grow from them. In order to protect the identities of those
involved in their pasts, the names and details of some
storytellers have been withheld or changed.

INTRODUCTION

What do you do when you find yourself sitting in the pretend comfort of your own life, yet wreckage is all around you? And your life is careening out of control? When addiction has overtaken you or abuse chained you with fear? Perhaps you wonder if your depression will ever leave or if relationships will ever be healthy again.

Your life can change, and it is possible to become a new person. The seven stories you are about to read prove that people right here in our town have stopped dying and started living. Whether they've been beaten by abuse, broken promises, shattered dreams or suffocating addictions, the resounding answer is, "Yes! You can become a new person." The unexpected collision that will cause you to break free from gloom and into a bright future awaits you.

Expect inspiration, hope and transformation … expect to be beautifully wrecked! As you walk with each real person from our very own city through the pages of this book, you will not only find riveting accounts of their hardships; you will learn the secrets that brought about their unexpected collision. These people are no longer living in the shadows of yesterday; they are thriving with a sense of mission and purpose TODAY.

May these stories inspire you to be beautifully wrecked.

DANCE MOVES
The Story of Marco
Written by Richard Drebert

So beautiful.

Betty's brown eyes were moist with emotion. She was just 16 when we first met at juvenile detention camp. She dated someone else then, another gangbanger.

"Do you take this man ...?"

Betty's smile grew intense, like she had suddenly unwrapped a rare pearl. She yearned for things to be decent and right between us, and I wished I could be closer, to reassure her.

"I *do*," she said.

"I now pronounce you man and wife."

I opened my fist and placed my fingers upon the prison side of the bulletproof glass. Betty's hand "touched" mine on the free side and lingered a few seconds.

Only nine more years to go.

I wondered if Betty was thinking the same thing.

"I love you ..." she said, and our telephone wedding at Donovan State Prison ended.

"Marco, it's time." The door buzzed, and I shuffled back to my cell. All that was sweet and clean in my life lived on the other side of my prison bars. I flopped on my bunk, with little thought of Betty's devotion or how she might struggle raising two children alone.

Instead, I contemplated conjugal visits.

❧❧❧

At Wagenheim Middle School, I strutted like a gangbanger. The teachers blamed my intensity and bad grades on ADHD (Attention Deficit Hyperactivity Disorder), and I couldn't care less. Dad took me off Ritalin, because it caused me to act docile and slow.

In middle school, I craved trouble to get attention. My teachers couldn't control me. Class attendance matched my attitude toward authority — rotten. Yet, I had a high degree of focus on one interest that few could touch.

Break dancing.

To spin, to *rage* in motion, set my heart on fire. On the dance floor I was creative. On the street I could compete. I reached excellence, the girls hung on me and my crew, my people, loved my style.

Dad's belt never hung far from my behind when I was at his house. He loved me but hated my street look. He worked hard at an electronics factory and tried to talk *his* sense into me.

"Your mama and me never raised you this way! How you gonna find a job in those baggy pants? Here, put these on ..."

Dad brought his heritage, language and preference in food with him from the Philippines. I got his Asian looks, but not his work ethic, until after I got out of prison. So, when I needed new clothes, I camped out at Mom's apartment. She took me shopping and let me choose low-slung, wide-pocket jeans and windbreakers. My white

Pumas spun in the air break dancing or slapped the sidewalk with my Asian gangsta strut.

My father had married my mom, a Caucasian girl he knew from the factory, who was a hard worker, too. They raised my brother and sisters and me in San Diego, until they separated when I was still hopping curbs with my Huffy. My Grandpa Lolo, on Dad's side, stepped up to fill in the gaps in my growing-up years. Filipinos stick together, and members of my family kept coming to San Diego from the Islands. Every year, Dad and my uncles got all the cousins together for a swimming party at Wild Rivers Waterpark at Irvine, to get acquainted with some and reacquainted with others.

Mom and Dad lived 15 minutes apart, so I jockeyed between the two, usually after an argument with one or the other. Mom was most flexible, so when I needed something, I stayed with her. Dad was stable, and I felt connected to my heritage through him and Grandpa Lolo, who came from Laguna, Philippines. Once in a while, like on Easter, we attended Good Shepherd Catholic Church in Mira Mesa. I got exactly nothing out of religion and held onto a vague knowledge of God for emergencies. Dad was the one I turned to if I was in trouble that I couldn't get myself out of.

A short, black-haired, wiry Filipino with boundless energy, in sixth grade I discovered break dancing. Driven by the approval of my crew, break dancing became my obsession. Night and day I practiced, until by seventh grade, I had perfected moves like the Nickel and the Yogi.

Each series of moves shrieked adolescent savagery at an adversary. I spun like a nickel, twirling on my shoulders and back, faster and faster, elbows and knees like knife points, Pumas beating the air above me in violent motion. Then flipping to my chest, I spun even faster to the deep bass roar of a boom box and whoops of the crowd. The smoother, the faster my spins and transitions, the greater the ovation.

Far different than performing on stage or in a basketball game, my break dance humbled my opponent, a fight without fists. An ultimate putdown that I craved to inflict.

I learned to battle a challenger with my eyes, then crush his spirit by spinning on my hands, with knees between my arms. The crowd gave way as I gyrated round and round, "walking" my body on the floor, like an insane top.

But my friends started losing interest in dancing to express their aggressions. I felt it, too, like it didn't touch manhood like *true* violence could.

I grew surly and antagonistic toward my teachers. Dad couldn't reach me anymore with his lectures, though he tried. I reveled in disrupting classes and finally ditched them altogether. I was too cool to be around losers and, with other boys, hung out in a secluded park across from the school to smoke.

Older guys, gang recruiters, came by now and then. "Wassup? Hang out with us, man. Hey, you wanna get jumped into our gang? We're TOC."

DANCE MOVES

Tiny Oriental Crips.

They kept their number of members to about 50 13- to 17-year-old kids and ruled our section of town. My friend and I were 13 and ripe for our first beat down. Three older boys surrounded me, and I defended the best I could. I came out without a broken nose or closed-up eyes, so I felt pretty good about it.

After a little backslapping and laying down the rules, we sauntered off proudly, official gangbangers. I had an identity now, and the deep cigarette burn in the top of my hand branded me TOC for all the world to fear. Break dancing was done. We only kicked it with our gang, swilling Olde English and learning how to jimmy locks to steal cars.

I learned Muay Thai (kickboxing) and loved to beat a rival gang member into the pavement. I memorized the faces of those I hated and held a grudge for months at a time. By eighth grade, the Wagenheim principal kicked me out of school altogether. It was Mark Twain High School for me, and everyone knew what kind of kids went there: troublemakers. Now I was with my own kind in one big room full of kids at various levels of "drop out" and ready to ditch again. Some of us wasted no time and ditched this alternative school.

A little older, and with my rep as a fighter, I sought out other gangbangers to challenge, especially if I caught OBS (Oriental Boy Soldiers) or AC (Asian Crips) drifting into our territory around Linda Vista Recreation Center, a sprawling complex of exhibits, parks and buildings. Police cars and cops on bikes trolled along the alleys and streets searching us TOCs out and busting us every week for curfew violations. Dad got pretty fed up with picking me up at the San Diego police station, but no amount of lectures deterred me.

Like a feral cat, I stalked the streets, passing churches touting Sunday sermons on billboards. Their messages invited me to touch God's mercy, but I needed none. I pursued a reputation: to be respected. Feared. It was Marco who would offer mercy, and only if *I* chose. I sold my soul to gang life: my cult of ruin.

I graduated from curfew violations to ride-alongs in stolen cars and ended up at juvenile detention. Strip searched. Frumpy blue jumpsuit. Dawn wake-up call. I hated the drill at first, but learned the routine like it was middle-school gym class.

"Where you from?"

"OBS."

"I'm TOC, you …!"

My fist found my rival's jaw, lightning quick and brutal. But *no joy* when the guards shot my eyes with pepper spray to separate us. After brawls, I spent days in cell confinement. Older TOC gangbangers praised my hair-trigger hatred, and I lived for their kudos.

When I stood before a judge charged with aiding in a car theft, he appraised me through big black bifocals. He gave me a lecture, like Grandfather Lolo, and I laughed at the slap on my wrist.

For most teenagers, "going to camp" means meeting

friends, swimming and hiking. After sentencing me for joyriding and other lesser crimes, authorities warehoused me at Camp Barrett until they could bust me as an adult, which seemed my destiny. At camp, when I wasn't laboring under supervision by staff, I tested my kickboxing skills against other gangbangers. Each sentence at the camps ended after about six months or so, and after my release, I lost no time in catching up with my TOC gang at Linda Vista Rec.

I lived most of my adolescence on probation and filled a cell in juvenile detention facilities and camps eight times before I was 18. I scoffed at probation rules and learned to boost Asian-brand cars with pricey stereos and wheels. After joyriding all over town, my TOC and I left the stripped car smelling of beer and pot and searched for another ride. Stereos and rims from the stolen car I pawned, sold or traded to other gangbangers.

At 14, I stopped riding with my homies and took the driver's seat, speeding down alleys and hiding behind buildings to evade capture by the San Diego police.

∽∽∽

"Marco! Come here!" My father had been trolling all evening to find me and hollered across an expanse of lawn at the rec center. I tossed away my cigarette and met him a little apart from my friend.

"You can't be out past curfew! I don't want to pick you up at the police station again!"

I humored him, one eye on my friend, who was grinning and hiding our bottles of beer. I promised to be home soon, just to get rid of him.

I hated the thought of facing my father at home and wandered the park alone for a while, tender quarry for venders of corruption.

"Hey, Marco! You wanna hang out?"

"I gotta go, maybe later, Hu." The young Asian who hailed me was gaunt from drug addiction.

"Got any money? Got something you'll *really* like, man."

"I have about 50."

"You gotta come! I mean you gotta! You won't be sorry."

I didn't want to go home, anyway.

Hu hooked me up with my first hit of meth, and I swooned in a dimension that stole all reason from my head. I never went home at all — for three months. I lived on the streets, stealing and fighting for my gang and smoking every night at meth houses. I might have been hooked for life, except for my cold-turkey stints in juvenile lockups.

Serious charges against me gained steam in the California courts, and staff at Camp Barrett knew I was bound for hardcore detention facilities soon. I knew Barrett like a favorite family camping spot, while I edged closer to actual prison.

I was 17 when I spent my last nine-month stretch at Barrett. Near the middle of my sentence, an Asian girl came by on visiting day and sat at a table with a friend of mine from Linda Vista. Betty was her name, and I couldn't get her out of my mind. I got her address and started writing her. We shared a lot about our lives, until losing touch during my months in detention.

At 17, I valued the approval from my TOC gang above my freedom to live according to my *own* dreams. In my soul, good and evil jibed like vile rap, and I danced to both, as if they were the same song. Betty lived with her brother and mother who couldn't speak English. Her mother depended upon her, and Betty yearned for stability for her baby daughter.

At 17, when I got out of detention, Betty and I spent time together, and we fell for each other. Something about her sent my priorities spinning off course. My father's values unexpectedly invaded my selfish heart, like a gang taking over new territory. But, sadly, Betty loved a gangbanger whose confused dream to start a family would hit a dead end.

When I flipped a borrowed Honda Accord after a high-speed chase, my life suddenly slipped into overdrive. By the time the Accord settled on its top, 10 police cars surrounded us. Besides the three of us, cuffed and lying face-down on the pavement, cops found a few rocks of crystal meth and an automatic pistol. I was still on probation, but my older friend, Dan, had warrants for his arrest and one strike against him in adult court already. If he copped to carrying a piece, along with a fresh drug charge, Dan would go to Donovan for several years.

I was still a minor with no strikes. In my experience, I believed that I would get a light sentence at CYA (California Youth Authority).

Evading arrest, reckless endangerment, possession of a firearm, possession of a controlled substance, probation violation: I took the blame for everything to keep my adult friend out of prison.

After sitting in juvenile detention for months, my plea deal for seven years at CYA wasn't so bad ... but then another charge suddenly caught up with me. And this charge carried a strike: I would be charged in adult court.

Months before, an AC (Asian Crips) member had thrown up a gang sign in my face, and I slammed him, ready to beat him humble. Suddenly five other AC surrounded me, and I ran for my car. I grabbed a heavy mag flashlight and chased down the original offender, hitting him one time in the head. Blood splattered everywhere, and satisfied, I left the scene. What I didn't know was that my license plate had been seen at the parking lot. Cops were looking for the car, and in time, authorities linked the assault to me.

Assault with a deadly weapon.

Because it was my first crime as an adult, the judge sentenced me to serve eight months in prison when I turned 18 and take one strike.

It seemed like a slam dunk for me, and I was ready for my first fieldtrip to Donovan. But before I served a day, my attorney sat me down, smiling, like he had just won a bet.

"The prosecutor offered you another deal, Marco. If you take one strike and stay on adult probation for three years, you can walk out of here tomorrow. They'll close the book on your case as soon as you turn 18 in two months. You're free, man! All you have to do is keep your nose clean."

Right.

The San Diego streets sucked me in like fumes to a crack pipe. I kicked my crime sprees into high gear, boosting cars and stripping goodies. Top gangbangers were getting to know my name. I had a strike on my record; I was a felon and proud of it. I sold a little meth on the side, but supplied most of my friends for free — my TOC loved to see Marco coming. And when a war broke out with COC (Crazy Oriental Crips) or OBS, I was first to fight. My gang chose me to splatter fear at their hangouts with drive-by bullets.

Within my violent gang insanity, I loved Betty and baby Lena. I was still clueless on how to be a father, a breadwinner or loving family man when Betty gave me wonderful news.

"You're going to have a son, Marco!" She touched her tummy, and I felt proud of my manhood.

In spite of my arrogance, a seed of reality took root in both of us, and Betty's love would lead me to the mercy I had rejected my whole life.

સ્ર સ્ર સ્ર

The gangbanger wore a bandana. He was older, a member of the Crazy Oriental Crips, and he looked at me *wrong*.

Our gangs were mortal enemies on the streets of San Diego, and I made certain I cruised by him real slow, so he could see that his disrespect made no impression. For Bandana, my disrespect invited serious payback.

I drove away, unconcerned, and his lowered Integra trailed behind me. I stopped at my house, but he kept rolling past.

"Baby, I'm on the way to pick up some cash from the Pioneer equipment I sold. I'll be back in a little …"

"I'm coming!" Betty already had the door open. Our daughter was with her mother, and I couldn't resist Betty's big smile.

As I hit the main street, a low-rider wheeled in behind me, and I cursed at Bandana who was with another COC member as passenger. They followed close, and I braked briefly for a stop sign. Even before the low-rider came to a complete stop, the passenger leapt out and swung a baseball bat at the side glass where Betty was sitting. He missed it clean as I sped through the stop sign and disappeared into a maze of side streets. I drove back to our apartment.

I had escape routes staked out wherever I lived, so I stole into a back alley and left the car running. I burst through our apartment door, where Lena lay in a crib. I glanced at her and at Betty's mom, who watched me curiously.

"Don't worry …" I said and grabbed a .38 from under my bed. I rejoined Betty in the car.

Betty's eyes snapped at me, round and fearful. "What are you doing, Marco?" I threw the gun on the seat between us.

"Hey, it's just in case …"

Bandana was waiting for us. At the first corner he tried to block our way out of the alley, and I opened up on him. After four shots, Bandana sped away, and I chased him a couple blocks, firing two more. He had threatened my pregnant wife, and I was dead serious about securing *his* disrespect.

Not a single bullet hit his car, but one bullet lodged in a fence. I knew that cops were drawn to gunfire like moths to headlights, so we hid out at a friend's house, planning to sneak back home. The car wasn't mine and needed to be returned to Betty's relative by 8 p.m., so I gave her the keys.

Betty and a friend drove off to deliver the car, and I sat down for a beer. Two hours and several beers passed, and I worried a little. I called to find out if Betty had returned the car.

"Marco, I thought you said you'd give me back my car by 8! Where are you?"

"You mean you haven't seen Betty?"

"Nope. What's going on with my car?"

My poor Betty. Bandana's wife had called the police, and while Bandana made his statement to officers, Betty had crossed at the very intersection where they parked.

Cops had pulled her over at gunpoint. Handcuffed and crying, she called me from the police station.

"Marco, they want you to turn yourself in. Please, you better do it. They said you can see me one last time before they take you …"

"Baby, I can't. I got one strike on my record, and they'll put me away for a long time! Just tell them what happened. It's okay."

She did, and they hauled off my precious 17-year-old pregnant Betty to juvenile detention where she spent months in a cell.

Two days after shooting at Bandana, the San Diego Police Department conducted gang sweeps in Linda Vista and picked me out of a carload of Asians. At gunpoint officers ordered me to place my hands on my head, fingers locked together.

The cops *knew my name.*

കകക

I faced a 10-year prison term in a California state prison. Betty was pregnant and spent three months waiting for sentencing as an accessory to assault with a deadly weapon. She skated with one strike on her record and a period of probation, because it was her first offense. Betty moved back into the apartment with her mom.

As for me, my crime flung me into hardcore incarceration. I waited for sentencing at the San Diego County Jail, overflowing with gangbangers like me. They all seemed to be looking to make a name for themselves, too. I had to watch my back every day.

In county jail, with no booze or meth to deaden my feelings, I sometimes attended chapel where I figured God lived. Most inmates had Gideon Bibles lying around, and I found one to read. I even went to prayer group sometimes, but my guilt, as heavy as a manhole cover, weighed upon my heart.

"I now pronounce you man and wife."

Minutes after our vows, Betty watched the steel door slam shut behind me, her life and mine separated by years of uncertainty.

❧ ❧ ❧

"Congrats, man. Any word when they're moving ya'?" my cellmate asked.

"Not yet. You been to Donovan. What's it like?"

"Not bad, if you know people. They'll hook you up."

I knew a lot of guys at Donovan State Prison. I had ridden stunt bikes with some of them as a kid. Boosted cars. Probably tried to kill some.

I'd do fine in Donovan.

Two months after our jailhouse wedding, I entered the California state prison system to serve out my 10-year sentence for assault with a deadly weapon, one year off for "time served." At Donovan, I adapted my gang persona to fit doing hard time. I settled into the protection system, segregated into heavy-handed racial divisions: Asians,

Blacks, Hispanics, Whites. In state prison, no matter who I wanted dead or humbled — if they were Asian, we were brothers, ready to defend against the other races.

As a felon, I *was* somebody. When I got out of prison, gangs on the street would know my name. All I needed to do was survive my stretch and follow the rules inmates laid down; go to work at the shoe factory every day; eat, sleep and do it over again — for nine years. I was 18. At 28 years old, I'd walk out of prison with plenty of life left to live.

Betty would come visit me. Now we were married, so I could expect even more from her. My daughter and son would come, too, and they fed my soul in ways I dared not admit to anyone in prison. Inmates would think I was weak.

But like a bar of prison soap, Betty's visits got thinner, until my family became only a sliver in my painful exile. In quiet moments, when I asked myself *why* I filled prison shoes at all, I knew that I had driven Betty away.

"I know you're doin' stuff! Don't lie to me!" In Donovan, I boiled in a human soup of suspicion and jealousy.

I knew how to curse an enemy with my eyes. On the streets, I cut a rival gangbanger to pieces with my stare of disrespect. Now Betty felt the curse.

"How can you say I'm untrue, Marco?"

Dragging our two kids on a 30-minute odyssey through San Diego traffic to see their felon father was grueling. Betty had enrolled in nursing school and, at the time, still managed to visit me. I rewarded her loyalty by accusing her of betrayal.

Over the years, our hopes for keeping love alive cooled, like the hot rubber in the prison shoe factory. Our longings cured to bitterness, and like most inmates, I tossed our dreams of a lasting relationship onto the pile of failed prison marriages.

ॐॐॐ

Every inmate at Donovan is required to get a diploma, and I studied to get mine. Unlike living on the streets and constantly fighting for status, I had time to reflect upon my future. I no longer had to preserve gang respect, and I observed the lives of inmates around me. Hard cases sneered at Christians for being weak, but I couldn't help but envy their courage in speaking about their faith. And these "believers" seemed to be genuinely peaceful about serving their sentences.

Within the routine of my prison years, I began to wise up about my life. Pride had seduced me to seek respect on the streets from gangbangers who had the same agenda as me: to make a name for themselves. Reality slammed me hard at night as I lay in my cell bunk. Fear of not being tough enough to live on the streets again troubled me, while I reflected upon the people closest to me: my mother, who loved me without reservation; my father, who worried over my violent nature; my wife, who hoped that I might become a good husband and father.

My family cared about me, unlike my TOC friends who were in business for themselves. During Betty's visits (now mostly for the kids' sakes), I reached out, trying to reconnect and rebuild the fledgling trust we had once shared. But was it too late?

I was 27 years old when I made a choice to leave TOC. It was only God's mercy that my Betty let me back into her heart.

"Hey, Marco. God loves you, man." At the gym, Christian guys kept saying it to me as I lifted weights, counting down the days before my parole.

"Why don't you give your life to Jesus before you get out?"

"I'll think about it …" I told them.

I could do anything if I set my mind to it, including go straight.

Just before I got out, an old guy, still street savvy, took me aside. He looked serious as he shook his head, remembering his own life. "Marco, whatever you do, don't try to catch up with the time you lost while you were here in prison. It'll get you in trouble."

ॐॐॐ

Betty looked like she had just stepped out of a fashion magazine. I felt drained, after hours of processing: 3 a.m. wake-up call. Four hours at Receiving and Release for paperwork and clothing. My state-issued 200 bucks, and then the long walk to the prison shuttle. All morning I had been assailed by fears: *What if I do something wrong and the warden revokes my parole?*

Betty saved me. At the Su Casa parking lot, I hopped into her car, and she drove to two different schools to pick up our children: Elementary school for Jason, and middle school for Lena.

Surprise! Daddy's home from prison!

Shopping. My first fast food in 10 years. Then *home.*

To sleep in my own bed, to eat breakfast with my family, I felt like a new man! I set up dates to meet my parole officer and started trying to find work. I didn't try to avoid my old friends, many of them former felons and gangbangers. Betty had rented a new place for us, and she didn't want to cramp my style right away, so she got a babysitter and went to the clubs with me. I was in the mood to celebrate, and it lasted months.

It felt good to be free, and I turned 29 at the On Broadway nightclub, *trying to catch up with the time I lost while in prison.* On Broadway was a fun place to hang out — and a meeting place for a church. Ironically, clubbers partied on Saturdays, and church folks came in to talk about God on Sundays.

The bouncer knew me: I had started a fight weeks before, and he expected trouble again. It was 3 a.m., and Asian gangbangers staggered outside the club in little groups. I could barely stand up, and I felt the fighter coming alive inside me. I had made a name for myself. I had done 10 years. No one messed with TOC or *me ...*

Suddenly a police car sidled up to the curb, and two

officers spoke to the nervous bouncer, hands fiddling with their pistol grips. The officers glanced around at a few well-known members of TOC and at me. A bystander mentioned I was on parole … and a policeman called it in. I stared, blurry-eyed, at him.

"You're under arrest for violating parole …" I heard the cuffs wheeze and snap, and he pushed my head down as I flopped into the back seat of the police car.

Betty watched the cruiser pull away. Mascara ran down her cheeks as she cried her eyes out. *Gone again.*

꙰꙰꙰

Receiving and Release again: I knew the drill and felt like scum. It wasn't cool this time, nodding to inmates as a surly prison guard herded me to my cell. The iron door slammed and locked, and I slumped on my bunk, dead inside.

This time, eight months.

My nightmare had just begun. Usually I could slip into a routine. I had schooled myself to survive any ordeal. Not this time. I had lost everything! Betty's tear-stained face haunted me, and memories clawed inside my head. I remembered my children laughing as I poured orange juice on school mornings. I had promised to buy them bicycles and take them to the Wild Rivers waterslide. Now their dreams lay shattered, like Betty's best tea set, stomped to pieces by Daddy. Would they ever forgive me?

"We knew you'd be back. Missed Donovan, huh?" The

jokes by other inmates jabbed at my wounded conscience.

Like sludge in the sewers beneath San Diego, guilt deepened in my soul. I had failed my son and daughter and sabotaged Betty's hopes for a fresh start in our marriage. Was there anything that could clean up my mess?

I jump-started a conversation with God in my cell. "Lord, I'll be with you one day ..." Every morning, my cell door racked open, and I marched to breakfast, robot-like, encased in a hopeless shell. Week after week, I tried to hit my old prison strut, but instead, I stumbled all over my failures. A sliver of hope slipped through a single crack in my world: Betty still visited me. My promises came fast and furious as I faced her through bulletproof glass, uncertain that I could keep any of them.

Something new reflected in Betty's eyes. Ultimatum. Resolve. I didn't care; at least she was here! I'd commit to anything, if I could have just one more chance. Just the *possibility* of forgiveness softened my selfish shell.

As the months ground by, another voice pierced my old routine of self-preservation. Tom served time for drug dealing and worked with me at the shoe factory. He was Guamanian, and I studied him as he poured rubber into shoe molds. His face wasn't tight. He didn't seem to be on guard constantly or fearful as he walked through the lines for chow. We pumped iron at the weight pile, and it was almost like he was already *dead*. He didn't jockey for status or get angry if anyone cursed at him for speaking his mind.

"I love Jesus, man. That's all. He took away all my pride, and I'm stronger now."

We talked and prayed together sometimes, and it felt like Tom was slowly digging me out from beneath an avalanche of fear I had been buried in. Suddenly, I could breathe, just a little.

"God can do it, bro. He can save you and put your life back together. He has the power. Put your life in his hands."

Sometimes I ignored him, and he quit digging. Then I'd ask a question, like "Whatcha think happens when you die?" and he'd scrape off a layer.

"The Bible says *I'll* go right to Jesus, Marco. Where'll *you* go?"

తతత

Near the end of the longest eight months of my life, my sister-in-law, Tina, invited Betty to bring Lena and Jason to an Easter egg hunt at Canvas Church in Little Italy.

Moms stood around watching children gather colorful eggs, and a few people approached Betty. "Come to church next Sunday. We'd love to have you! There's lots to do for your kids."

"Oh, we're just here for the Easter eggs!" Betty said cautiously, but the caring invitations struck a beautiful note in her heart.

Betty's sister, Tina, encouraged Betty to give Canvas a try, and a week or two before I got out of prison, she attended services there. She felt a strange satisfaction in her soul as she listened to Pastor Ben talk about Jesus. Tina had dived head-first into the exciting Canvas Church scene and planned to have her two children dedicated to God.

After the guards processed me out of Donovan, Betty was waiting for me again at the Su Casa parking lot. I felt humbled, like someone had pounded me with quicker, harder punches, but at least I was free.

At home, Betty told me, "We aren't doing any more clubs, Marco. No more drinking. We're staying HOME!"

I nodded, and in my heart I said, "Yes, ma'am." This girl was my connection to goodness, and I would do anything to keep her.

"We're gonna live like hermits, Marco!"

In a month, I landed a job at an auto body shop. I stayed off the streets, trying to adjust to life on the outside of prison, under new "Betty Rules."

One day, Tina asked us to attend a ceremony that showed the world that her kids belonged to Jesus, for life. I couldn't believe my own ears when I told Betty I would go to Canvas Church with everyone, for Tina's sake. I really *was* changing.

Canvas Church. That name seemed so familiar ...

The very air I breathed at Canvas' rented school building seemed to throb with joy. Not like the On Broadway Club, where people laughed 'cause they were stoned.

This was happiness from the gut, real and shared. Tina

stood at the podium with Pastor Ben, and he prayed for her little ones, while my emotions came apart.

I kept wiping away tears that leaked out of my face, while layers of pride and selfishness loosened up inside me. After songs, Ben preached, and I heard *some* of it — but another powerful voice spoke over his.

It was Jesus.

He told me he loved me. God said he was setting me free from my past, so I could live the way he designed me to live from the beginning. He took all my wasted life upon himself, and I felt the weight of fear I had carried my whole life *disappear.*

As I sat beside Betty, I couldn't stop crying out for God to forgive me. At the end of Ben's sermon, Pastor asked if anyone wanted to give his or her life to Christ, and I raised my hand. I walked forward, with my beautiful Betty, thinking that this wasn't "church" like I remembered it as a kid. At Canvas, I connected with God for the first time!

Our family started attending church whenever the doors were open, and I didn't feel like I had to watch my back anymore. At Canvas, Betty and I found true friends, some like me, who had come out of gang life on the San Diego streets. They shared their freedom with us, and we began moving to the powerful new rhythm of God's Spirit.

My marriage began to change, too. After I gave my life to the Son of God, I suddenly could *hear* Betty and respond to her needs better. My children took Jesus as their Savior, too.

One day, I figured it out. That weird feeling that I

knew the name, "Canvas Church" — Tina told me that Pastor Ben used to hold church services in the same building, before On Broadway became a nightclub. The Canvas Church banner hung on the wall, an ironic signpost directing a Filipino gangbanger where to find God.

చ్చాచ్చాచ్చా

Miracle.

Betty and I are learning to trust God and his people, beyond our life experience, and God is showing himself strong in very personal ways. In this hard economy, the auto body shop cut my hours, and it's not easy for a former felon to find work. Friends at Canvas prayed with us, and someone directed me to a contractor who hires ex-felons to work for the U.S. Navy ...

"Marco. We need 20 buckets of non-skid to the top floor!"

Carrying 100-pound containers of liquid flooring up flights of stairs seems endless. Up to 70 hours a week, I tear up and replace decking on Naval ships at the San Diego port. I'm in good company. Most of my co-workers are as glad to be working as I am.

Betty works two jobs as a CNA, and our young marriage, so tattered from past mistakes and failures, is a miracle of God's creative healing. I feel no need to hang with a gang, protecting a neighborhood so I can feel useful. I have a purpose and goals. God is opening up new opportunities, and *he* protects my family and me.

Ten buckets to go.

Aching legs and shoulders are nothing compared to the anguish of losing everything a man dreams about. For this "old" break dancer, former gangbanger and ex-con, Jesus is rewriting my whole story — while I'm still a young man.

I follow no one but Jesus now, and he is teaching me dance moves that no one can shake loose.

LOVE SONG
The Story of Katie
Written by Karen Koczwara

"Katie, I know you're in there!"

My heart stopped as I heard my mother's shrill voice on the other side of the door. She couldn't be here, not now!

"Mom, you've gotta get out of here," I hissed, flinging open the door. "It's not a good time now." Frantic, I glanced back at the closed bedroom door, where Gabe sat measuring out the meth on the other side. I couldn't let her see us like this.

"What's in the bedroom?" she pressed, pushing past me.

I tried to block her as I thought fast. "Gabe's changing, Mom. Please, you need to leave." My voice rose as panic crept into my chest.

"Katie, I just …" My mother's eyes were pleading, her face wrought with concern as she stared at me. I knew what she thought … her little girl, once so full of promise, now a shell of a person with sallow skin and a hollow stare. She wanted me back, but it wasn't that simple.

"Mom, you have to get out of here," I said firmly, pushing her out the door.

"Katie, please," she begged. "I love you, and I want to help you."

On impulse, I reached up and slapped her across the face. "I hate you, Mom! Get out of here!"

My mother reeled in shock, whirled around and ran to the car. Moments later, I watched her screech out of the parking lot, sideswiping a pole as she veered around the corner and disappeared.

Instantly, my heart sank. *What have I done? Oh, what have I done? What sort of a monster have I become?*

I had stooped to a new low, and I hated myself for it. Hated the person I'd become, hated the world I'd been sucked into. But I was in too deep; how could I ever escape now?

๛๛๛

I was born in Olympia, Washington, in 1975 and grew up in the tiny town of Yelm in Western Washington near our extended family. My brother, parents, relatives and I enjoyed weekend get-togethers and barbecues on special occasions. My early years were idyllic, but when I was 11, my world was rocked to the core one horrible night.

I had just settled into bed upstairs when I heard my parents yelling down the hall. Groggy, I sat up and listened as the fighting grew worse. I couldn't make out their words, but they sounded very angry. Moments later, I heard the front door slam. Tears spilled down my cheeks, and I knew in my heart that my father was gone.

The next morning, my mother called my brother and me into her room. We sat on the edge of her king-sized waterbed, our bare feet dangling over the edge as she quietly spoke. "Daddy has left, and he is not going to be coming home," she said, trying to keep her voice steady. "He loves you very much, and none of this is your fault."

I trudged down the hall to my room, where I burst into tears. No matter what she had said, I still wondered, *What had I done? Could I have been a better daughter?* In my mind, my father had not just left my mother ... he had left *me*.

There is never a good time for a father to leave, but my father's absence was especially untimely as I entered middle school and moved into the awkward, hormonal pre-adolescent years. My brother and I visited him on rare occasions.

"Your mother wanted this," he grumbled over dinner. "I just don't understand why; I've tried everything."

I swallowed hard. "Dad, please, that's enough," I mumbled, stirring my food around my plate. I still didn't understand exactly why they got divorced; I only knew that things had never been the same since. I wished I could snap my fingers and make it all better again, but it was too late.

In 1988, my mother remarried. I liked my new stepfather well enough; he was funny and pleasant and tried hard to get to know my brother and me. But I decided from the start that I'd keep him at a distance; no use letting in someone else who might also leave us.

My eighth grade year, I joined a co-ed basketball team; I was one of only two girls on the team. The other girl, a student named Tiffany, approached me with a little white pill one day before practice.

"What's that?" I asked.

"Speed. Just like the name implies, it'll make us run real fast on the court. Here, take some," she urged, shoving it at me.

I finished lacing my shoes and took the pill. If it helped us run faster and compete with the boys in practice, what was the harm?

My freshman year of high school, I attended the homecoming football game. As I hovered near the bleachers with my friends, a cute guy sidled up to me. I'd seen him around campus several times and knew he was a popular junior.

"Hey, I'm Gabe," he said with a smile.

I was thankful it was too dark out for him to see me blush. "I'm Katie."

We chatted for a few minutes, and when he walked away, my friends squealed and giggled. "Oh, my gosh, Katie! He's, like, only one of the most popular guys on campus! Can you believe he was talking to you?! He totally likes you!"

"You think so?" I tried to stay cool, but inside, I screamed with delight.

Gabe and I began dating that year, and I enjoyed the attention he lavished on me.

It felt good to walk around school with a cute guy on my arm. The other popular guys took notice of me, too, and included me in their activities.

"You're Gabe's girl, aren't you?" they asked, waving and smiling as we passed in the hall.

Shortly before I turned 15, I gave myself to Gabe, losing my virginity to a guy I thought could give me the world.

Gabe and I dated all through high school. He began attending parties on the weekend, but I stayed home. My parents were strict and had instilled good morals in me.

"A nice girl like you doesn't need to be out partying on the weekends," my stepfather insisted.

After Gabe graduated, he started accusing me of cheating on him with different guys at school. "Look at that skirt you're wearing," he said in disgust one day. "You're just trying to get guys' attention, aren't you? I know you're messing around behind my back."

"No, I'm not!" I protested adamantly. "I swear, Gabe, you're the only guy for me."

My senior year, my parents loosened up a bit at home. When graduation rolled around, they gave me permission to go on a senior trip to Disneyland. "We know it's a once-in-a-lifetime opportunity," my mother said. "We want you to have a good time, Katie. Just be careful."

I headed to Southern California with three of my best friends for a week of fun, relaxation and adventure. Gabe called every night during my trip, still accusing me of being unfaithful. "I bet you're all over the surfer guys down there," he sneered.

"No, Gabe! Why won't you believe me? I'm just having fun with the girls!" I retorted.

One evening, halfway into the trip, my friends sat me down. "Katie, we need to talk to you. Gabe's been cheating on you. For a long time now. In fact, he messed around with me a while back," one of my friends told me apologetically.

"What are you talking about?" I cried, my voice rising as I grew hysterical.

"And there's more," my friend added with a sigh. "He deals drugs."

"Drug dealer?!" I screamed. "Are you kidding me?"

"I wish we were. I'm sorry, Katie, but the guy's a no-good scumbag," my friend said. "You really should get away from him."

I couldn't believe that the guy I'd been dating so long and given my heart and my body to had betrayed me like this.

"That's it!" I picked up the phone and called Gabe, my blood boiling. "Gabe, we're done. I know who you are and what you've done, and I don't want anything to do with you anymore!" I cried. "Just get out of my life." I was heartbroken, but I tried to stay strong and enjoy the rest of the trip. When I got home, I returned the promise ring Gabe had given me. I desperately needed to get out of Yelm, enjoy a fresh start somewhere else.

I applied to Seattle University and was accepted. That fall, I left behind my small town, my family and all I had known and prepared for a new life in the big city. For a girl growing up surrounded by cows, rural roads and farms, Seattle was a bit of a culture shock. I settled into a dorm downtown near the bustling Capitol Hill; sirens, horns and blaring music soon replaced the chirping crickets I'd fallen asleep to all my life. I'd asked for big change, and I'd gotten just that.

"I'm here to have fun," I told my new roommate, Meredith. She was a cheerleader and introduced me to a few people on campus. Within no time, I was invited to parties, where the beer ran freely and the drugs were rampant. When a co-ed offered me some marijuana, I didn't hesitate. Before long, I added cigarettes into the mix. My weekends were now full of booze, smoking and partying with new friends.

One spring afternoon during my freshman year, Gabe called out of the blue. We hadn't spoken in almost a year. "I'm in town and wanted to see if you were up for hanging out," he said casually.

Why not? I told myself. I still liked Gabe, despite what he'd done to me. He was fun, and "fun" was my new motto these days. We got together one evening, and when I went home for spring break, we met up again.

After cruising around one afternoon, Gabe drove his car up behind our old high school and pulled something out of a bag. "You ever tried coke?" he asked.

I shook my head. "No. Weed's all I've done," I replied.

"First time for everything." He winked as he laid out a line for me. "Just snort it like this." He demonstrated. "Ten times better than the high you get from weed."

I snorted my first line of coke, and from that moment on, I was hooked. I returned to college, and Gabe and I began dating again. On the weekends, I made the hour-and-a-half trek back to Yelm to visit him, often taking back roads to avoid anyone I knew. I kept a low profile while back in Yelm, hanging out at Gabe's house and doing drugs.

Gabe soon gave up coke and focused on meth. "It's the same high, only cheaper," he said.

"You gotta weigh it before you divide it into the baggies," Gabe explained, showing me how to measure the meth on a scale before separating it into the baggies. I followed his lead, careful to measure everything out equally.

I liked being his sidekick, but even better, I liked the way I felt on my new drug. When I was high, I could stay awake for days.

One evening, after delivering a few bags at a gas station, we heard sirens behind us.

"Sh**," Gabe muttered, glancing in the rearview mirror. He tossed the rest of the bags at me. "Quick! Shove 'em down your pants! Just do it!" he hissed.

Panicked, I obeyed and shoved the drugs down my pants. He pulled over, and a cop strode over to our window. "Looks like you've got a tail light out there," he informed us.

As the cop drove away, I turned to Gabe angrily. "How could you make me do that?" I cried. "What if we'd been caught?"

"It won't happen again," Gabe assured me. "I'm careful, Katie, I promise."

That summer when school got out, I spent all my free time with Gabe and his family. His father and brother used meth as well, and we all "tweaked" together in his house, the blinds closed and the lights off. When I was high, I wrote pages of elaborate poems, grew paranoid and began hallucinating. One evening, I stumbled into the bathroom and found Gabe at the sink, picking at his skin.

"What are you doing?" I asked.

"Bugs. I've got these crazy bugs all over me," he replied.

"Oh, man. Nasty."

I went home that night and brushed past my mother, slipping upstairs to my room without talking to her. She followed me, and I avoided her eyes, hoping she wouldn't notice how high I was. "You okay?" she asked.

"Fine," I replied, forcing a smile.

I stayed up all night and began picking at my skin, convinced I was covered in bugs as well. I spent the rest of the summer with Gabe, doing drugs and partying until school resumed. "Let me take some back with me. I'm gonna need it when I've gotta cram for classes," I pleaded.

"No way. This stuff stays with me. You know where to find me," Gabe said firmly.

I returned to school a shell of a person. I'd lost a considerable amount of weight, my skin was pale and my hair dull and stringy. When I ate too much, I felt disgusting, stuck my finger down my throat and made myself throw up. I developed a destructive pattern of bulimia, and my body began wasting away. When I returned home, my family noticed my skeletal appearance and became concerned.

"Are you anorexic, Katie?" my mother asked one night, her eyes sad as she tried to talk to me.

I shook my head. "I'm fine, Mom. You know how college is, stressful and stuff."

A few months into my sophomore year at Seattle University, I realized I might be pregnant. "Have you taken a test yet?" my friend Jessica asked when I shared my fear with her.

"Not yet." I bought a pregnancy test and slipped into a stall in the communal bathroom in the dorm. My heart raced and my hands shook as I waited for the results to show up. Within minutes, two pink lines appeared on the stick; I was officially pregnant. In shock, I ran off to find my friend.

"I don't know what to do," I cried. "I'm so scared! I'm too young for this!"

Jessica was quiet a moment. "Well, my friend got pregnant a while back, and she went to Planned Parenthood. They took care of it there."

Took care of it. I knew what this meant. I didn't want to be pregnant; was this the answer? I went back to my dorm room and thought long and hard. Gabe was nowhere near ready to be a father, and I still had three years left of school. I couldn't deal with this now; I had too much going on.

I visited the local Planned Parenthood a few days later. After taking another test, the nurse confirmed I was indeed pregnant. She handed me a stack of pamphlets. "This should tell you everything you need to know," she said matter-of-factly.

I took the pamphlets numbly and flipped through them. They explained the abortion procedure and what to expect. "So, now what?" I asked.

"We need to do an ultrasound, and then we can schedule you for the procedure," she explained.

How ironic, I thought as I lay on the ultrasound table. I had chosen Seattle University because they had an excellent medical program, and I'd always wanted to be an ultrasound technician. My mother was in the medical field, and I thought it would be fun to be the one to announce the gender of the baby to expectant mothers. Now here I was, pregnant, knowing deep down that the results I awaited wouldn't produce tears of joy.

The technician turned the screen away from me so I couldn't see what she found. "Mmm hmm," she mumbled under her breath as she made some notes on a chart. "All right," she said at last, setting down the wand. "Here's the number you can call to terminate your pregnancy. They'll get you all set up."

Two weeks later, I stepped into the abortion clinic. "Unfortunately, since you're so far along, we need to insert something in your cervix to make the procedure easier," the doctor explained.

I gulped hard. This was getting a bit more complicated than I wanted. I went home, panicked, and told Gabe everything.

"I'm freaking out," I blurted. "I just want this to all go away!"

"I'll pay for the abortion," Gabe replied coolly. "It's all gonna be fine."

On the day of the procedure, Gabe picked me up and drove me to the clinic. Fear overcame me as I stepped through the doors and sat down across from a nurse. "Do you understand what you're about to do?" she asked calmly.

"Yes," I replied quickly.

"Have you considered anything else?" she asked next.

I shook my head. "No."

I lay frozen on the hard, sterile table and tried to ignore the different sounds as they began the abortion. *It will all be over soon, and you can get on with your life,* I told myself. After it was over, the nurse strode over to me.

"Do you want to see him?" she asked quietly.

"See who?" I asked, confused.

"The baby."

"No!" I cried, angry and disgusted. Why on earth would I want to see the baby? Why would she even ask such a thing? I was fuming as I shuffled back into the waiting room. Gabe gave me a hug and helped me to the car. I sat in the front seat, staring straight ahead at the road as he drove me back to school. I was completely numb.

"You okay?" he asked as we pulled up at my dorm.

I nodded. "Fine." I retreated to my room, where I lay on my bed and burst into tears. I was thankful my roommate was out as I sobbed into my pillow, holding my stomach to ease the cramping. *It's over; you should be happy,* I told myself. Then why did I feel so terrible?

Too distraught to return to my classes, I spent the next few days in my room. I hated my life, hated myself, hated Gabe for being so nonchalant about the whole thing. To make the pain go away, I returned to Yelm that weekend, knocked on Gabe's door and did a few lines of meth. *It's all over now,* I told myself. *I can go on with my life.*

From that moment on, I decided I didn't care about anything. I stopped going to class and turned to meth when any sort of emotions returned. One evening, as I helped Gabe line up the meth in the back bedroom of his apartment, I heard my mother's voice in the front room.

"Katie? Where are you?" she cried. "I know you're here!"

I stormed out of the bedroom. "What are you doing here, Mom?" I demanded.

"What's in the bedroom?" she asked, trying to push past me.

"Mom, you can't go in there! Gabe's changing," I lied, panic rising in my chest. I knew my mother was concerned about me, but I couldn't let her see what really went on over here. I pushed her out the front door. "Come on, Mom. You need to leave now."

My mother stared at me, her eyes sad. "Katie, I love you, and I want to help you," she whispered. "Please let me in."

On impulse, I reached up and slapped her across the

face. "I hate you, Mom! Leave me alone! I don't want you here!" I screamed.

Reeling in shock, my mother raced to her car and sped off, sideswiping a pole as she careened out of the parking lot. I stood on the porch, shocked at myself and what I'd just done. What sort of horrid person had I become?

Devastated, I walked down the street to the nearest grocery store, where I called my stepfather from a pay phone. "Is Mom there?" I asked slowly.

"Yes, she's here," he replied tartly.

"Is she okay? I heard her hit something on the way out," I said.

"She's home. The car's not okay, and she's not okay, but she's safe."

"I love you," I whispered sadly as I hung up the phone.

I walked back to Gabe's, overwhelmed with disgust at myself for what I'd done to my mother. She'd been nothing but kind to me over the years, always trying to reach out and help, and I'd returned her love with a horrific slap in the face. *How can I ever forgive myself?*

I returned to school and tried to pull myself together, but it was difficult to focus in the midst of this terrible turmoil. Gabe grew abusive with me, often shoving me against the wall and yelling insulting remarks when I didn't do as he pleased.

The man I thought I'd once loved was becoming a monster, but I was too afraid to leave him for good.

෩෩෩

LOVE SONG

In March 1995, unable to cope, I dropped out of school. I found a studio apartment in downtown Seattle and tried to decide what to do next. Gabe's abusive behavior continued, and he began cheating on me again. One evening, after a huge fight at his place, he decided to leave for the weekend. As I sat in the empty apartment, alone and distraught, I decided I was done. I'd hurt my family, I'd become the puppet of a terrible man and I'd just thrown away a bright future by dropping out of school. *It would be better if I wasn't here,* I convinced myself.

I emptied an entire bottle of pills into my mouth, lay back on the bed and waited to die. I awoke to Gabe shaking me violently. He dragged me to the bathroom, where he tried to make me throw up before shoving me out of his house. "I won't have you die here!" he screamed as he pushed me out the front door.

I stumbled to my car and managed to drive down the road. I was in a complete daze, and the roads were dark and winding. Though I didn't black out, I had no recollection of anything after that. When I woke up, I was on the floor of my new apartment. Panicked, I rubbed my eyes and tried to stand up.

What on earth happened? How did I make it here? And how am I still alive? I was angry I hadn't died. "Why did you do this to me?" I cried, shaking my fist at God. I didn't really believe in God, but if by some chance he'd had anything to do with all this, I wasn't happy about it in the least.

Shaken to the core, I crawled to the phone and called my mother. "I need your help, Mom. I need to get out of this lifestyle. And I need to get away from Gabe for good," I pleaded.

"All right. We're going to get you through this," she replied. "You need to stay strong. Just call Gabe and tell him you want nothing to do with him anymore."

My heart raced as I dialed Gabe's number. I knew him too well; he was going to be furious. "Gabe, I'm done with you. Stay away from me!" I told him firmly when he answered the phone. My whole body shook as I hung up the phone. *Please, please don't let him come after me. Let him leave me alone in peace so I can move on. I just can't do this anymore.*

One day, while my friend from the university came to visit, Gabe showed up out of the blue. As I chatted with my friend in the living room, Gabe jumped the tiny fence below the high-rise apartment. He stormed up to my place, where he banged on the door. "I'm gonna kill you, Katie!" he screamed. "You made the wrong choice kicking me out of your life, and you're gonna be sorry!"

"Get out of here, Gabe!" I screamed back. Frantic, I called 911. It was the last time I ever heard from or saw the monster, and to my relief, he left me alone for good.

I moved out and found another apartment in Redmond, Washington, where I got a job as a receptionist for an Australian software company. My life became a monotonous routine of work and sleep. Every day after work, I went straight home, flipped on the TV and ate dinner alone. I had cut all ties with my old life and my drug friends, but I now had no one in my life. *I'm okay,* I told myself. *I don't need anyone.*

On Monday mornings, I overheard my bosses talking about how they'd gone to church. "We had so much fun at that potluck yesterday," one lady said. "I can't wait to do it again!"

My bosses were warm, caring and friendly people, and I was envious of the life they lived. *I wonder if all people who go to church are that happy,* I mused.

My mother called one day to check on me. "Remember your old friend Michael?" she asked. Michael was a girl I'd known back in high school; we'd played basketball and volleyball together. "She needs a place to live for a few weeks out near you, so I gave her your number. I hope that was okay."

"Sure, I guess so." *It might be nice to have some company around here,* I decided. *It's awfully quiet in the evenings.*

Michael moved in with me, and I enjoyed getting to know her again. She went to church, too, and often talked about God. I'd never set foot in church in my life and didn't have much interest in spiritual things. I kept on smoking cigarettes and drinking and began pining for meth again. One evening, I called up Gabe's brother in desperation. "Can you get up here and bring me some drugs?" I pleaded.

"Katie, you know I can't do that. Gabe will kill me if he finds out I'm even talking to you," he replied.

I sighed. "Whatever. Fine." I'd just have to rely on the cigarettes and booze to numb me for now.

"You should come out with me and my friends tonight," Michael said one night. "It will be fun. We're gonna go catch a movie."

"No, thanks. I'm good." I patted the couch. "Got my beer; that's enough for me."

A few minutes later, to my surprise, Michael returned with her friends. "Since you didn't want to go out, we brought the party to you," she said with a smile. "We grabbed a movie. Hope it's okay." She gestured toward the guys. "You know my boyfriend, Jeremy, and this is his friend Ben."

I glanced up at Ben, taken aback by his striking brown eyes, tall stature and cute smile. "Hi," I mumbled. "Nice to meet you."

Ben and I chatted that night, and I instantly liked him. He played basketball and was extremely funny and easy to talk to. *He's so cool and so cute,* I told myself. I hadn't felt this way about a guy since Gabe first made me swoon at that football game years ago. Why was I getting so flustered? Wasn't I supposed to be enjoying my new solitary life?

A week later, Jeremy invited me to Ben's birthday party. I showed up and was impressed with how friendly all of their friends were. Unlike the friends I'd known, they knew how to have fun without getting high or drunk. Ben and I talked all night, and I decided I liked him even more. He was completely opposite of Gabe in every way, and to my relief, he wanted nothing to do with me physically.

"Isn't God good?" I overheard one of the guys say as the night went on. "He's been teaching me some really awesome things lately."

"Me, too," another guy chimed in. "I can't wait for church next Sunday."

I listened intently as they discussed church with the same enthusiasm my bosses at work did on Monday mornings. Maybe I was missing something on this whole church thing. It might be nice to just check it out sometime, see what all the fuss was about.

Saturday night, Ben called. "Just wanted to see if you and Michael wanted to go to church with us tomorrow," he said.

"Hold on." I sat down and relayed his words to Michael. Everything inside me screamed, "Yes!" but I didn't want to appear too eager.

Michael laughed. "Katie, go to church? You really want to go?"

I sighed. "You're right. That's probably a joke." I returned to the phone. "No. Thanks, anyway," I told Ben as I hung up.

I went into my room, closed the door and flung myself on the bed, sobbing. I so badly wanted to go to church, but maybe I didn't belong there after all. How could a bad girl like me be accepted in a place like that? Michael was right; I wasn't the church type.

The following Saturday night, Ben called and invited us to church again. This time, before I could consult

Michael, I screamed, "Yes!" I felt like a giddy school girl getting ready for a first date as I rushed around the house, pulling together my best outfit for the big day.

"I'm so nervous," I told Michael. "I don't know what to wear, and I don't even own a Bible."

"You're fine," Michael assured me.

I woke up with butterflies in my stomach the next morning. After checking my attire in the mirror half a dozen times, I finally headed out with Michael. As we entered the church doors, the pastor and his wife strode over to greet us with a warm handshake. "So glad you are here today," they said. "Thanks for coming."

I slipped into a seat next to my new friends and stared ahead at the screen above the stage. Upbeat music began, and people raised their hands, clapped and sang along. I clapped along, too, and jabbed Michael in the side. "This is amazing!" I whispered.

She just smiled and shrugged as if to say, "No big deal. We do this all the time."

The pastor spoke about Jesus as he read from the Bible. "Jesus spent his time on earth with outcasts, rejects and the poor," he said. "He showed love to those who had never been shown love, and he died on the cross for those who did not yet know his love. You, too, can experience and know that love and peace he brought to this earth. Jesus loves *you*."

Everyone clapped as the service ended, and I sat glued to my seat, still mesmerized by it all. I'd loved every minute of church, from the second I walked in the door to the closing song. I could hardly wait to go again and learn more about this Jesus the pastor spoke about.

I showed up at the Wednesday service and then attended the following Sunday as well. The more I went, the more intrigued I became. Deep down, I knew this was what I'd been missing all my life. There'd been something different about Ben and his friends the minute I met them, something I couldn't quite put my finger on. But now I was almost certain I knew what that was: They loved Jesus.

One weekend, my new friend Sybil invited us all over to the place where she was house-sitting. "We can all hang out," she said.

Ben showed up, too, much to my secret delight. As we chatted, I shared with him how excited I was about church. "That's awesome, Katie, but have you ever asked Jesus into your life?" he asked.

I stared at him. "I've wanted to for so long, but I don't know how!" Tears streamed down my face.

"All you have to do is say a prayer. Here, we can pray it right now. You can bow your head and pray along with me if you want." Ben closed his eyes and began. "God, I come to you and ask for your forgiveness. I know I've done wrong in my life, and I want a fresh start with you. Please come into my life and be the center of everything I do and say."

I prayed along with him, meaning every word in my heart. For the next three hours, I could not stop laughing. "This is amazing!" I cried. "I can't believe it! I feel freer and happier than I have in my entire life!"

"That's God's presence in you," Ben explained. "He's filling you with his peace as you give your life to him. Isn't it exciting?"

"So exciting!" I gushed. For years, I had tried to fill the holes in my life with parties, drugs, booze and guys. Now, I could see I only needed one thing: I needed Jesus. He was the only one who could make me whole, the only one who could offer true joy. The girl of my past, so broken, lonely and depressed, was gone now, replaced by one with a new song in her heart. There was no turning back now.

Ben gave me my first Bible for Valentine's Day, and I was beyond grateful for this precious gift.

"Where do I start?" I asked, overwhelmed as I slowly turned the pages.

"The book of John is an excellent place to start," Ben suggested. "But, really, all of it is pretty good," he added with a smile.

He also gave me my very first Christian CD by Jars of Clay. I listened to "Love Song for a Savior" over and over, sobbing as the words echoed the ones in my heart:

> Someday she'll trust Him and learn how to see Him.
> Someday He'll call her and she will come running
> and fall in His arms and the tears will fall down and she'll pray,
> "I want to fall in love with You."

I flipped open my Bible one night and read, "Lord, my God, I called out to you for help and you healed me … you spared me from going down to the pit … you turned my wailing into dancing … and clothed me with joy" (Psalm

30). As I mulled over these words, I suddenly realized why God had saved my life the night I'd tried to end it all. He'd had a plan for me, and that plan included knowing him. I may have been in the deepest of pits, but he had pulled me out, healed me and given me a joy I didn't know was possible. I now had a reason to wake up in the morning, because I had purpose in him.

As I learned more about God over the next few months, my heart began to break for the things I'd done. I knew I was forgiven, but I also knew I'd hurt many people, including my family. I owned up to what I'd done to those closest to me and asked for their forgiveness, but my huge, horrible secret still remained. Could God really forgive me for aborting my own child?

One night, I cried out to God, asking him to help me forgive myself for what I'd done. "The Bible says you've forgiven all our sins, no matter how great. If you've forgiven me, I know I need to forgive myself, too, God."

But I didn't know how I'd tell Ben what I'd done. If he knew about the abortion, he'd probably run the other way.

My friendship with Ben grew, and I soon realized we were much more than good buddies. One morning at church, I glanced up at him. His hands were raised as he sang from his heart straight to Jesus, and I distinctly heard God say to me, "I didn't just bring him into your life so he could introduce you to me. This is the man."

The man, God? As in, the one for me? Tears sprang to my eyes as I watched Ben. He truly was the man of my dreams, so unlike anyone I'd ever met before. But how could this wonderful guy, a pastor's kid, want anything to do with a messed-up girl like me? There were so many other nice girls at church he could be dating. *Why me, God?*

I got more involved with church and the college ministry, and others from the church came alongside me to mentor me in my new relationship with God. "I really believe that God has a special plan for your life," one pastor told me. I quit my job as a receptionist and decided to go back to school to become a teacher. I worked at a bagel shop in the evenings to pay the bills and moved into a cute two-bedroom apartment with a roommate. My world felt more complete than ever; I had a new set of friends who loved God, a great guy and a new direction in life. I could only attribute it all to God's grace.

I wasn't sure I could be any happier, but as it turned out, I was wrong.

❧❧❧

"Where is he? I thought he was just going down the street for Chinese food," I mumbled to myself. I glanced up at the clock impatiently. It was my 21st birthday, and Ben wanted to spend the afternoon in the park on Lake Washington with me. He'd gone for Chinese food and said he'd be right back, but he was taking an awfully long time.

Finally, he showed up at the door. "Sorry it took so long," he apologized. "You ready?"

As we set out a blanket near the lake and dug into our food, I decided I couldn't think of a more perfect way to spend the day. I missed my family, of course, and wished they could be here to celebrate. We'd always organized big get-togethers for special occasions over the years. But I was here with the man I loved, and that was what mattered most.

"Here, open your fortune cookie," Ben said, tossing it to me.

"Oh, I'm stuffed. I can't eat one more bite," I replied.

"C'mon. You have to read your fortune. It's fun," he insisted.

I cracked it open and pulled out the paper. "Katie, I love you. Will you marry me?" it read.

With tears in my eyes, I gazed up at Ben in disbelief. "Of course I will!" I cried.

He got on one knee, pulled out a ring and slipped it on my finger. I cried as I gazed at the sparkling many-faceted diamond representing his love and commitment. *God, what have I done to deserve this man? He is so perfect! Thank you!*

"I already drove down and asked your mom and dad for permission to marry you, so don't worry, the deal's sealed," Ben added with a grin.

"You're too good." I laughed. "This is the best birthday ever!"

The "best birthday ever" got even better when a limousine showed up a few hours later. As Ben led me back to the banquet hall at a fancy restaurant, I was shocked to see my entire family sitting there. "Happy birthday, Katie!" they yelled. Tears sprang to my eyes as I glanced around at my loved ones, all here to celebrate with me.

I turned to Ben, amazed. "You did all this?" I whispered.

He nodded sheepishly. "Yeah, it was all me. Happy birthday, Katie."

Ben and I married a year later on a beautiful, sunny August day. Three months after we wed, I confessed my abortion to him. My heart raced as I shared my story, but Ben spoke only kind words to me. "Katie, God has forgiven you. Why would I not forgive you, too?"

I was relieved to have my secret out in the open. God truly loved me just as I was, and so did my husband. I was free from my past and the burdens that had entangled me for so long. As our pastor said, I was a new creation in Christ, a whole new person. I may not have spent the first 20 years of my life living for God, but I had the rest of my life to serve him.

As Ben and I prayed, we felt God asking us to take a year off work and school and do an internship at the church. My family was disappointed by our decision and didn't understand why I'd risk my financial future to serve God.

"If my daughter's happy and healthy, though, I guess that's all that matters," my mother concluded. I prayed one day they all would find the peace and joy I'd discovered by knowing God.

Ben and I enjoyed our internship as we worked with various ministries in the church. We took several trips to San Diego and fell in love with the warm climate and the friendly people. We prayed and felt God leading us to move there to help with a new church in the area.

"I know we're really stepping out of our comfort zone, but I am sure God will provide for all our needs," Ben said confidently.

We talked to our family and friends, asking if they would help us any way they could to cover our bills for the first year, and in 1999, we made the big move down south. Ben became a licensed youth pastor, and after our second year with the church, they hired him on full-time. I graduated from college with a degree in Biblical Studies and Education and took a job as an assistant director at a learning center in Escondido. In 2002, I gave birth to a beautiful little girl, Cara, and in 2004, another sweet daughter, Faith.

Our life felt more complete than ever, but the adventure was just about to begin.

෨෨෨

In 2005, Ben and I moved to Las Vegas to help start a youth program at a church there so kids and teens might have a chance to hear about Jesus' love sooner than I did. During this time, we felt God leading us to become full-time pastors of a church. In 2008, we returned to San Diego, the place we now felt was home, and continued to ask God to make it clear where he wanted us to be. In February 2009, we held our first service at Canvas Church in downtown San Diego. Our desire was that people from all backgrounds would find authentic friends, genuine support, love and, of course, the truth of the Bible when they walked through the doors. I thanked God for the gift he'd given Ben as a pastor and for fulfilling the desires of our hearts to reach out to the community we loved.

My heart started to be pulled toward women who, like myself, had had abortions. I knew the church so often talked shamefully about it instead of dealing with the brokenness that results from aborting a child. I began an abortion recovery group and was thrilled to be able to share my story of healing with others.

"If you've had an abortion, you are not alone. I know the pain all too well and have experienced God's great healing in my life," I told my new friends in the group. "God showed me the verse in Psalm 30, which says that he turns our wailing into dancing. If you are in the midst of pain, God can turn that sorrow into joy and put a new song in your heart as he did in mine."

As I drove home that night, the stunning San Diego sunset fading behind me on the 5 freeway, I belted out my favorite Jars of Clay song. "I want to fall in love with you …"

I had much to be thankful for — our wonderful daughters, Canvas Church and, of course, my beloved husband, who'd taken a chance on a messed-up small-town girl with a broken heart.

LOVE SONG

Ben had loved me just as I was and had introduced me to someone else who did, too … Jesus. My life was my love song to God, my gift to the one whose grace was bigger than the wounds of my past.

I sang for him, because he loved me.

FIGHTING FIRES
The Story of Michelle
Written by Karen Koczwara

How will it feel to get shot in the head?
Will I die instantly?

These are the two thoughts that race through my mind as the gunman points his pistol at my temple, nudging the steel barrel into my skull. I've never imagined I would die like this, here, in a parking lot on a sunny spring day.

"Hand me your wallet!" he barks.

I should memorize his face, his clothes, his hair color, but I don't. Instead, I keep my focus on the steering wheel as I pass my wallet through the window. A strange calm overrides the panic that threatens to erupt from within. I hear my mother and sister's voices, inches away. They sound foreign and distant, too far to protect me from death. I am the one with the gun to my head. I am the one who might breathe my last breath.

Will I die instantly?

The gunman snatches my wallet and jumps in his van. He is gone. I remind myself I am alive. My heart is still racing, my palms damp with sweat, but I am alive. The nightmare has passed.

"Oh, Michelle!" My mother is crying in the back seat. I want to cry, too, but I don't. I hear my mother on the phone with the police. *Keep it together,* I tell myself. *You have to keep it together.*

I stare straight ahead, gripping the steering wheel like a life preserver. I can almost feel the pistol where it pressed into my skin just moments ago. The tears should come now, but I fight them. Later, I will collapse. But right now, I have to be strong for everyone else. It's my job. It's what I do. There's no time for crumbling now.

❧ ❧ ❧

I was born in Detroit and moved to Ann Arbor, Michigan, in 1978. A bustling college town, it boasts dozens of mom and pop coffee shops, cafes and bookstores downtown, as well as the prestigious Ann Arbor Film Festival and Art Show. Its quaint, picturesque streets suggest storybook perfection, and for many years, I tried to make my life perfect as well. But just as the icy storms come racing into town each winter, so did the storms in my own life, blowing off the mask I'd worked so hard to perfect.

My mother was just 18 when I was born. On the eve of my birth, my uncle burst into the nightclub where my father worked and shared the news.

"You're about to become a father!" he announced.

My father embraced his new role as a daddy and married my mother two years later. As they settled into life as newlyweds, my father gave up the wild ways he'd picked up at the club and stopped drinking and smoking. When I was 5 years old, my sister came along. Our family was now complete.

FIGHTING FIRES

From the time I was young, I excelled in school, pouring myself into my studies. I joined the cross-country and track team in junior high and was successful on both. On Sundays, I attended church, where my father served as a Sunday school teacher and my mother as a youth leader and member of the choir. From the outside, I was the poster child for a well-rounded American teenager. But behind the walls of my home, things began to crumble.

My parents, both from dysfunctional homes, fought often. Late at night as I crept off to bed, I heard them sling harsh words back and forth down the hall.

"What are we going to do now? You got laid off? How are we supposed to pay these bills piling up?" my mother cried.

I climbed into bed and tried to shut out the noise, but the yelling continued until I finally dozed off. If only I could make things better, make them stop fighting. In math class, the answers came easily, lining up in tidy rows across the page. But making two parents get along was more complicated.

My parents' fighting continued as I entered high school. One afternoon, feeling hopeless and depressed, I locked myself in our bathroom and popped open a bottle of pills. I decided I was going to end it all right then; life just wasn't worth living anymore. One by one, I dished out the pills, lining them up on the counter. I glanced up in the mirror and caught my reflection. I'd practiced my smile a thousand times for the world, but beneath my perky face lay a hurting girl who kept her secret pain locked inside. I scooped up the pills and was just about to shove them all in my mouth when I heard my little sister down the hall.

"Michelle! Come here!"

I knew that cry all too well; my sister needed my help.

"Michelle! Just come here!" she cried again, her voice shrill and desperate.

Sighing, I set down the pills and ran out to check on my sister. "What's going on?" I asked when I found her in her room, crying.

"I just need you," she said in a small voice, throwing her arms around me.

I thought about the pills and how close I'd come to ending my life. How could I have thought of such a thing when my sister needed me so much?

"It's gonna be okay," I whispered, reassuring both of us as I pulled her tight.

My parents separated my senior year; I was devastated by our broken home. I kept up my studies and focused on sports, trying to be the best athlete and student I could. Toward the end of my senior year, a cute guy caught my eye, and we began dating. I applied to Brown University and was accepted with a full-ride scholarship. With a boyfriend on my arm and a ticket to a prestigious school, my future looked bright and promising.

Just weeks after beginning at Brown, my sister called in tears. "I can't do it anymore without you here, Michelle," she sobbed. "I hate going back and forth between Mom and Dad. I need you here!"

"I'm so sorry, sis. I'm trying to focus on school. I'll come home and visit soon," I promised her.

But as the weeks passed, my sister became more distraught. Always one to try to hold the family together, I felt I had failed at my job as protector. I tossed and turned every night as I went to bed and often forgot to eat. Exhausted and defeated, I finally asked the school for a medical leave. I packed up my books and belongings and headed back home to care for my sister.

"When are things gonna get better around here?" my sister asked wearily. "I'm just so tired of all the fighting."

"I don't know, but I'm here right now," I replied. "We'll be okay."

Determined not to give up on school, I began classes at the University of Michigan just down the street from our house. My father worked on campus there, but our relationship was now strained.

One afternoon, I passed him on the way to class. Our eyes met, but we said nothing as we kept on walking. My chest tightened as I quickened my pace.

I wish things weren't this way, Dad. I wish you'd just worked it all out with Mom. Now look what you've done to our family.

I applied to Harvard University and was accepted. I finished out my degree there and returned to Michigan, where I bought a house and landed a teaching job. From the outside, I still looked good — graduate of one of the top schools in the nation, competitive athlete, a homeowner with a respectable job. To the world, I was the picture of success. But my insides continued to crumble as my depression worsened.

If I could not fix my family, what was it all worth?

↷↷↷

"I'm pregnant, Michelle." My sister called me one day with the news. "I know it's crazy. But I'm gonna keep the baby."

"Wow! Well, I'll do whatever I can to help you," I assured her.

My sister moved in with me after she had the baby, and I helped support them. We grew especially close during this time, but I knew I couldn't stay by her side forever.

I learned about a Spanish program in Costa Rica and decided to pursue it. Perhaps a fresh start in another country was just what I needed.

"I'm still just a phone call away," I reminded my sister as I packed my things.

In July 2005, I met a cute guy named Eric in the Spanish program.

"Where you from?" he asked one day after class.

"Michigan," I replied. "I needed a change of scenery."

"Well, you've come to the right place. Seventy-five degrees year round," he said with a smile. "I'm from San Diego, California."

Eric told me he was divorced and shared custody of his two young children, Luke and Lori, against his ex-wife's will. We quickly grew close, and just two months after we began dating, he proposed. I moved to San Diego with him, and we talked about starting a business. Eric was a big drinker; I often came home to find an empty bottle of vodka in the trash and him relaxed on the couch. I had never been much of a drinker and didn't particularly like this habit, but I brushed it off.

We all have our things, I told myself.

One evening, Eric suggested we go to a strip club together. "It'll be fun," he insisted.

I shrugged. "Why not?" *At least we're going together,* I reasoned.

A few weeks later, Eric came home with some movies. "Thought we could have a special private viewing," he said, flashing them at me.

"Porn?" I sighed. "All right, sure. It's all harmless fun, I guess, right?"

As he popped the video in and the images came on the screen, I shifted uncomfortably on the couch. *What am I doing? First strip clubs, and now porn? I'm supposed to be the good girl, the girl whose dad taught Sunday school.* But just as quickly as I thought this, I reminded myself of the man my father had become. *Maybe it was all for nothing,* I told myself. *What does it all matter, anyway? What's the use in trying to do everything right?*

Eric and I married and settled into life as newlyweds. We loved San Diego, with its warm climate, bustling downtown and miles of sandy beaches. We started a corporate transportation business transporting clients in limousines and vans; we were excited to watch it thrive. But at home, our marriage quickly grew rocky.

Shortly before our first anniversary, I noticed Eric's drinking escalate. One evening, I came home to find him stumbling around the house, a bottle of vodka and a jug of orange juice on the counter.

"What are you doing? Are you making screwdrivers again?" I demanded, snatching up the bottle and tossing it in the trash. "You're wasted!"

Eric passed out on the couch a few minutes later. Angry, I stormed off to bed. As I lay there fuming, something else gnawed at me. Eric had been spending a great deal of time with another girl. He insisted they were just friends, but their relationship bothered me nonetheless. *He wouldn't do something behind my back, would he? Can I really trust my husband? Am I just being paranoid?*

Eric's brother and his wife were pastors of a local church. They invited us one Sunday, and I agreed to show up. The moment I walked through the doors, I felt as though I'd come back home. It had been years since I'd set foot in church; after high school, I'd lost all interest in anything to do with God. But as I listened to the pastor speak, something stirred in my heart.

"God wants you to come as you are," he said. "He doesn't care where you've been or even what you've done yesterday. He simply wants you to seek forgiveness and move forward with him. His grace is bigger than your past."

I chewed on these words over the next several weeks as I continued to attend church. The God the pastor talked about not only forgave us when we asked, but also *forgot* our wrongdoings. Was it really possible God could forgive all I'd done? After all, I'd watched porn, gone to strip clubs and had sex before marriage. I thought of my own father, often slow to forgive when I messed up. "You say you forgive me, but you keep bringing it up," I'd often lamented to him growing up. Was God really different than the father I'd known?

The more I attended church, the more I became convinced it was what I'd been missing in my life. *I need a relationship with God. He is the only one who can heal my broken heart, the only one who will keep his word, the only one who loves me just as I am.*

I prayed one day, inviting him into my life.

"God, I know we haven't talked in a long time, and honestly, I'm almost afraid to pray to you after all I've done. But the pastor says your grace covers all things, and I choose to believe that you will forgive me if I turn all my junk over to you. So here I am, asking for that fresh start, asking for your forgiveness. Thank you for loving me and for being my heavenly father, even though my earthly father has let me down. I now know you are all that I need."

For the first time in my life, I understood God's undeserved kindness and believed he was offering it to me, freely. The minute I invited him into my life, I knew things would never be the same. My shameful past was just that — my past. My heart today was all that mattered to God. I prayed that in time Eric would find that same relationship with God and discover the same freedom I'd found.

My sister met a wonderful man and became engaged to him. I was thrilled that she'd found such a good role model for her young daughter. I was even more excited when she asked me to be a bridesmaid in her wedding. We talked back and forth on the phone, discussing wedding plans and growing eager as the big day approached.

"I can't believe it! My baby sister is getting married!" I gushed. "I just got my bridesmaid dress. I'll see you in just a couple weeks!"

A week before the wedding, I got a phone call that rocked me to the core. "He's dead! He died of an asthma attack this morning!" My sister's voice was barely audible as she sobbed into the phone.

Dead? It couldn't be true. Just days from becoming a new bride, my sister's fiancée was snatched from her life? It felt like a cruel joke.

"I'll be on a plane as soon as I can," I told her. I fell to pieces the minute I hung up the phone. *Oh, God, how can this be? What will my poor sister do now?*

I flew back to Michigan, where I spent the next few days sitting with my sister, comforting her the best I could. I had no words for her; the simple cliché responses seemed pointless in the midst of such tragedy. My new faith in God was rattled as I watched my sister grieve. It was so unfair.

"Are you mad at God?" I asked her one night before bed.

She shrugged. "I'm mad, yeah. But you know what? My faith in him isn't destroyed. I don't understand why this happened, but I can't question his ways. I just have to trust that he'll hold me up and that one day all of this will make sense," she replied quietly.

I nodded. "You're right." In that moment, I realized that living for God did not mean life would be trouble-free. It only meant that we'd have someone to comfort us along the path. Trials did not mean he did not love us; instead, they were a chance for us to trust in him.

Regretfully, I had to get back to work, leaving behind my sister, still so distraught. "I'll be back in the spring," I promised.

I returned to San Diego and focused on our business, which was now busier than ever. Eric continued to drink, but I brushed it off. In April, I returned to Michigan as promised to visit my sister.

One afternoon after church, my mother, sister, niece and I went out to lunch. As we left the restaurant and headed toward our car, I suddenly heard an unmistakable voice in my head: "Something's wrong." I ignored it as I unlocked the car and hopped in. My sister climbed in next to me, and my mother and niece buckled up in the back.

Suddenly, out of nowhere, a man jumped out of a van next to us, yanked open my door and put a gun to my head. "Hand me your wallet!" he barked.

As the gun pressed against my skull, a strange mixture

of peace and panic overcame me. Immediately, two thoughts entered my head. *How will it feel to get shot? And, will I die instantly?* My heart racing, I reached into my purse and grabbed my wallet, handing it through the window.

The man kept the revolver pressed against my head as I stared at the steering wheel. My world grew very small as the two thoughts repeated over and over in my head. Some people talk about one's life flashing before their eyes when threatened with death, but there was no time for that now. I only wanted to know that if he pulled the trigger, I'd quickly die in peace.

"Give me the rest of your stuff!" he demanded.

I rummaged through my purse, my fingers shaking so badly I could hardly grab my belongings. I passed them through the window, and he finally released the gun, jumped back in the van and sped off. I leaned back against the seat, my heart thudding in my chest. My mother and sister cried softly in their seats, badly shaken.

"Oh, my gosh, Michelle! He could have killed you!" my sister cried through her tears. She leaned forward and managed to catch the license plate on the van before it disappeared down the street. As they sobbed around me, I held myself together, trying to be strong for us all.

"I'll call the police," I said evenly, grabbing for a cell phone. I dialed 911 and reported the robbery. Even as I relayed what had happened over the phone, I remained calm. *No time for breaking down now,* I reminded myself. *Later, I will fall apart.*

Next, I called Eric and told him what had happened. The tears then came in a flood as I spilled everything. "I thought I was going to die!" I cried. "It was so awful, Eric!"

"Oh, baby. I'm so glad you're all right. I'm so sorry, and I wish I was there. Come home, okay?"

I drove to the police station in a daze. Soft praise music played on the radio, and the words comforted me. I replayed the incident over and over in my mind as I gripped the steering wheel. Even on the brink of death, I'd still tried to hold it together for my family, tried not to let them see my fear. Suddenly, I realized I'd spent my whole life living this way, always rescuing my sister, comforting my mother, acting as the glue that kept us from unraveling. But talking to Eric reminded me that I enjoyed a life outside of my family, a life I could not ignore. My family was important, but I could not play the knight in shining armor forever, galloping up to save the day whenever tragedy struck. I could not take on the world; that was God's job, not mine.

"Okay, God, I hear what you're trying to tell me," I prayed. "I give my family up to you. Remind me to trust in you instead of trying to do it all on my own."

When I returned to San Diego, Eric noticed a change in me. "You're awfully quiet," he mused one day. "You okay?"

"Fine," I replied quickly. The robbery had shaken me but had also caused me to deeply reflect on my life. I felt like I'd flown to Michigan one person and come back as another.

I tried to articulate these feelings to my husband, but it was difficult, so I kept quiet.

Eric continued to drink, and I grew more concerned with his behavior. Our line of work in the corporate transportation industry often required us to attend networking events, where we took potential clients out to lunch. These clients sometimes included attractive young women. I didn't like this aspect one bit and became increasingly suspicious of Eric's infidelity. I wanted to believe my husband only had eyes for me, but deep down, I wasn't so sure.

By the end of 2007, the turmoil in our home grew worse. Eric's ex-wife was mentally unstable, and the custody situation with the children became complicated. Eric and I fought often, and I grew weary with our circumstances. When my mother hinted at wanting to move, I suggested she join us in San Diego and become our office manager.

"You know what? I'll do it," she agreed.

I was excited for the extra help and the opportunity to be closer to my mother. Five days after Christmas, Eric and I decided to take his kids on a spontaneous camping trip to the desert. We packed up our things and headed out of town, eager for a few days of rest after a whirlwind holiday season. Just after we reached the campsite, my mother called, hysterical.

"You're never going to believe this, but the business building is on fire!" she cried.

"What?! You're kidding! The whole building, Mom?"

"The whole building. One of your clients called me; he saw the fire from his house. I think you'd better get back here quick!"

"Our building is burning up! Our whole business is going to be ashes!" I cried when I got off the phone.

"What?! I need to get back there, right now!" Eric said frantically.

"It's going to take us forever to pack everything up. Why don't you stay back to get our stuff together, and I'll head back to San Diego?" I suggested.

"All right," Eric agreed.

I jumped into the car and breathed hard as I put my foot to the gas and sped back toward San Diego. As the speedometer climbed, I ignored the number, focused on only one thing. I had to save our business. Our whole life was in that place. If the building was destroyed, we'd be ruined, too.

By the time I arrived, the entire building was engulfed in flames. I stared in horror as they leapt from the building into the air, smoke coiling into thick black clouds above them. The firemen arrived on the scene and did their best to fight the fire. I jumped out of the car and raced toward the building.

"Please, I need to get in there! That's my business!" I screamed.

"Ma'am, it's dangerous," a fireman warned. "Stay back."

"Please! I need to get our cars out!" Our cars were our livelihood; we couldn't let them burn.

"All right," the fireman finally agreed. "We've got that side contained, so you've got time. Be quick, though."

My mother arrived at the scene with the office keys. "What do you want me to grab?" she asked.

"Anything you can! Computer stuff!" I hollered back. "Hurry!"

With the help of some friends, we managed to get all the cars out of the garage and drive them down the street to our friends' boat yard. I raced back in the office and grabbed some documents off the desk. My mother snatched our computer hard drive and server and met me out front. We stared at each other, trying to catch our breath as we watched the flames grow thicker.

"I can't believe this," I cried. "This is crazy!" As the adrenaline drained, I burst into tears.

"There, there. It looks like they have it under control. Why don't you go back home?" my mother suggested. "It's going to be okay."

I called Eric with an update. "Looks like things are under control. Stay put, and I'll call you soon," I told him.

I stumbled back to our condo just a few blocks away and collapsed inside. Suddenly, I heard a huge explosion. I flew to the window and, to my horror, watched our entire building explode down the street. "Noooo!" I screamed. Like a scene out of an action film, the flames shot up to the sky as though the building had been bombed.

And just like that, it was gone.

I threw open the door and ran outside, where other people from our building watched the horror unfold. My knees buckled beneath me, and I fell to the ground sobbing. "No, no, no," I murmured in disbelief. *How can this be happening? This must be a nightmare!*

Within moments, I heard more sirens and saw the fire trucks race down the road. Living downtown, I was accustomed to sirens blaring in the middle of the night, but tonight, the emergency was ours. Everything we'd worked so hard for was gone, demolished before my very eyes. How would we ever get back on our feet?

"Look what I grabbed," my mom said incredulously, holding up a folder. "It's the reservations for the New Year's Eve shifts! Maybe we can still pull it off!"

I sank onto the couch, trying to decide whether to laugh or cry. "You really think we could pull off New Year's Eve?" I asked, shaking my head. The holidays were the busiest time of the years for us; was it possible we could salvage what we had for the show to go on?

At that moment, I realized I could do two things. I could give up, or I could make the best of a terrible situation. I'd never been a quitter; my whole life, I'd stayed determined, and that determination had paid off. "Let's do it," I said, springing into action. I jumped to my feet, grabbed the car keys and headed off to Wal-Mart with my mother in the passenger seat.

"Look at us! We're a mess!" I laughed as we grabbed a cart at the store. I was covered in ashes, my face streaked with black smoke, my hair rumpled and my eyes bleary. We veered in and out of the aisles, grabbing soda and other necessities for the cars and the chauffeurs. I called our employees and instructed them to clean out the cars.

"We're back in business, boys!" I announced.

Eric arrived the next morning. By nothing short of a miracle, we dispatched all our drivers on New Year's Eve and made it happen. We set up shop in our condo for the next few days until we could find a place downtown to rent. Slowly, business returned to normal. We learned that the fire had begun at the demolition company next door to our garage; it had spread quickly to our place. As I replayed the past few days in my mind, I thanked God for his timing and provision. By his grace, we had salvaged the most important items. Our building was gone, but we were not ruined after all.

On the home front, however, the fires blazed out of control. Our finances grew tight, and the situation with my stepchildren and their mother worsened. Eric began spending time with a friend who was single, often going out late at night with him to drink. When I confronted him, he insisted he didn't have an alcohol problem.

"I'm just having a little fun. Since when is that such a crime?" he snapped.

In August 2008, while running a cross-country meet, I met a fellow runner. We began chatting and found out we had much in common. "You went to Harvard?" I said excitedly. "I went to Harvard! So cool!"

My new friend and I shared many other interests, including books, business and, of course, running. "We should meet at the track sometime," he suggested. "I'm always around on the weekends."

"Me, too," I replied eagerly. I gave him my phone number before we left. *Harmless*, I told myself. *I'm not attracted to him in the least. He's a lot older than me and definitely not my type. But maybe we can be friends. It's always nice to have a running partner.*

We began spending a considerable amount of time together. I enjoyed my new friend's company and our in-depth talks as we pounded the pavement each week. He was financially stable, raised Catholic and very well-rounded. The more we hung out, the more I realized how opposite he was of my husband. *I wish I could talk with Eric like this,* I lamented. Slowly, my affections grew for my friend, and though I still wasn't attracted to him, our meetings became the highlight of my week.

"I wish you'd just loosen up. Have a fling or something," Eric said casually one night after one of our many spats.

"Seriously?" I glared at him. "I can't believe you just said that! You know what? Fine! I'm going out!" I stormed out of the house and showed up at my running friend's house. We talked late into the night, and I finally fell asleep on his couch. The next morning, I returned home. It was Thanksgiving, a day to thank God for all of our blessings. Yet I felt anything but thankful these days. My life was falling apart; what was there to be grateful for?

"What are you thankful for?" my mother asked as we went around the table that afternoon.

"I'm thankful I'm alive," Eric mumbled, poking at his turkey.

"And I'm thankful for my health," I piped up. It was the best I could come up with.

❧❧❧

As 2009 approached, Eric and my relationship grew even more strained. I focused on the business and slipped on my running shoes when I needed to clear my head. I got more involved in church and volunteered to teach Sunday school. I desperately wanted to be close to God, but my circumstances felt hopeless. Could God still love me and really have a good plan for my life?

That spring, I learned Eric had slept with another woman after we got engaged. I was furious. "I knew it! I knew you were cheating on me!" I stormed around the condo, throwing my things into a box. "I'm outta here! I'm done with this crap!"

Shortly after I moved out, I slept with my running friend. I still wasn't attracted to him, but I was dying to be noticed and loved, and he returned my affections and made me feel special. Deep down, I knew I needed to turn to God with my hurts and my broken heart, but instead, I filled the emptiness with temporary gratification.

In June, I learned about a new church called Canvas Church in downtown San Diego. I decided to check it out one Sunday. The minute I walked through the doors, I felt completely at ease. The pastor and his wife welcomed me with a warm handshake and a smile.

"So glad you're here," they said.

The pastor's wife spoke about God and what he had done in her life so transparently that I felt I knew her by the end of the service. I still longed to be close to God and had not given up on him. Perhaps Canvas Church would be the perfect place to connect not just with God, but with others who were pursuing him, too.

At the end of August, I took a leisure trip to Nicaragua and El Salvador. When I returned, Eric and I hardly spoke. There was no hostility between us, but divorce seemed the only reasonable solution to our problems. Eric had no interest in being monogamous, and after fighting so long for our relationship, I was finally ready to give up.

"I know this man who's a minister down by you," my sister told me a couple months later. "Maybe you could talk to him and get some advice."

I met with the man and shared my story. I expected him to dish out the pity and give me permission to divorce my husband, but instead, he surprised me with his response. "If it wasn't for your ego, could you forgive Eric?" he asked.

I thought for a moment. "Maybe," I said at last. I loved Eric; I had always loved him. Could forgiveness really change the course of our relationship, or was it too late?

"A lot of times people assume the grass is greener on the other side, but that's not usually the case," he added with a smile. "If Eric is willing to do his part, God will honor you for forgiving your husband."

I could not afford to live in the city on my own and looked for a place to share with a roommate. I went to check out an apartment downtown and noticed a Bible on the girl's table when I stepped inside. "Do you go to church?" I asked her.

"Yup. Are you a Christian, too?" she asked with a smile.

We began talking, and I briefly explained my circumstances. She shared some words of comfort with me. "I'll be praying for you. Just keep reading your Bible and trusting in God. All things are possible with him," she reminded me.

Though the apartment location didn't meet my needs, I kept in touch with the girl and began using her as my hairdresser.

One day she asked me, "Michelle, what if you had to say it was your fault?" Her words took me aback at first, but as I thought it over, I realized that perhaps she was right. I *had* played a part in our marital problems. My mind wandered back to when I'd first met Eric and how easily I'd let him take us on a path of lust as we watched porn, visited strip clubs and talked about other women. What sort of standard had I set for myself and for my marriage? I hadn't set a godly example to begin with.

As the weeks passed, however, nothing changed between Eric and me. I grew discouraged and filed for divorce. Convinced I needed a change of scenery, I applied for a doctorate program at Harvard and was sure I'd get in. *I'll put this all behind me and move on,* I told myself. But to my surprise, I wasn't accepted. I was shocked and confused as to what to do next. Leaving San Diego had seemed like the simple solution; staying would be much harder.

I started talking to Eric again and praying about our relationship. "God, if there's any chance for us to salvage things, please show me how. I need your strength to love my husband and reconcile with him." I prayed about my own heart, asking God to forgive me for the wrong I'd done in our relationship. To the world, I'd portrayed myself as the victim and Eric as the bad guy. But I could now see that I had contributed to our demise as well.

"Eric," I said one night. "I'm really sorry for what I've done to cause you hurt. Please forgive me."

As I took ownership for what I'd done, Eric responded with a soft heart. "I'm sorry, too," he said. "I know how much I hurt you, and I hope you can forgive *me.*"

The more we talked, the closer we grew. My heart began to change as I recognized my role in our dissolved relationship. I'd spent a lifetime playing peacemaker with my own family, trying to hold us together when my parents went their separate ways. Yet I hadn't been willing to do that very thing in my own marriage, the relationship that mattered most in my life.

One night, Eric called and invited me to dinner and a movie.

"Sure, that sounds nice," I said shyly. As I got ready, I felt like a high school girl getting ready for a first date. Things were moving slowly, but we were connecting again, remembering why we'd fallen in love in the first place. Maybe there was hope after all.

Eric and I gave each other our hearts again, committing to work on our marriage and put each other first. He began making better choices with alcohol, trying to show me he'd really changed.

Our amicable friendship slowly transformed into romance, and I thanked God for the work he was doing in our lives. At last, I understood the difference between simply *doing marriage* and being a wife. I wanted to love and cherish Eric, and I wanted our marriage to thrive, not just exist. With God as the center of our relationship, this was possible.

After moving back in with him, I soon learned I was pregnant. The timing seemed perfect; we grew excited about adding a child to our home. I enjoyed the time I spent with Luke and Lori; perhaps a baby would bring our family closer than ever.

I went back to Michigan to visit my father. We had spoken more over the last few years, and I had forgiven him for the hurt he'd caused our family. On a Sunday morning, I began miscarrying. "No, God, don't let me lose the baby. Not here, not now. Please, if I'm going to miscarry, let it be in California with my husband," I prayed through my tears.

As I prayed, I felt a hand slip into mine and hold it up. When I glanced up, there was no one there, but I distinctly felt the hand in mine. One that could only belong to God, the ultimate comforter in times of trouble. A flood of peace washed over me, and I cried, thanking God for his presence.

FIGHTING FIRES

My stepmother stepped into the room and asked to pray for me. "Here, I have a verse for you," she said quietly, opening her Bible. She read Psalm 27:13 aloud: "I am still confident in this; I will see the goodness of the Lord in the land of the living." The words penetrated my soul and brought reassurance to my heart. God had restored my marriage; he would sustain me in this, too, and I would see his goodness through it.

I flew back to California, where I miscarried in the emergency room a few days later. Eric sat by my side, squeezing my hand as we grieved the baby we would never know. I was devastated but thanked God I had not endured this trial alone.

"It might take months to get pregnant again," the doctor told me.

I nodded. "We'll see what happens," I said, trying to smile.

Within a short time, I learned I was pregnant again. Eric and I were cautiously excited, but as the weeks passed, we grew ecstatic about a new addition. Meanwhile, Eric's ex-wife grew increasingly unstable and took us to court, claiming we were unfit parents for the children to stay with. She invented a slew of lies, insisting we'd forced the children to eat from the garbage and didn't let them have clean water. My first instinct was anger, but I took the situation to God in prayer, asking him to reveal the truth in court.

"God, please bless this judge with discernment," I prayed as we approached the bench.

To our relief, the judge found favor in us. Eric's ex-wife was stumped that her lies hadn't held up on the stand. On January 18, 2011, 10-year-old Luke came to live with us full-time. On January 23, I gave birth to a beautiful little girl, Elizabeth. Within a week, we became the parents of two children. I was thrilled to have a daughter and happy to be a positive influence in Luke's life. Little Lori loved baby Elizabeth, and I prayed one day she might be able to live with us full-time, too.

"I know I'm not your mother, but I love you," I told Luke one afternoon as I helped him with his homework. "Please let me know when you need my help."

We got more involved in Canvas Church over the next few months. I shared our story of reconciliation with the church and was transparent about everything, including the infidelity. For the first time in my life, I truly felt at home in a church. Canvas was full of people just like myself, all with past hurts and stories, all willing to be open about their struggles. The pastor preached with truth and love, reminding us that through God, we could find forgiveness and hope, not condemnation.

As I reflected on my miscarriage, my heart began to break for women who'd had unplanned pregnancies and abortions. I now simply saw them as hurting women who'd made a choice through their brokenness. That brokenness had led them to do something they might once have thought unimaginable, and it had ultimately crushed their heart in the process. I thought back to my affair and realized I'd done just that: I'd reacted out of a place of hurt in the midst of my husband's infidelity. In the end, we all need God's grace, forgiveness and cleansing in our lives. Only he could make us whole again.

"I know I've got a Masters in education, but I don't really feel like I'm supposed to be teaching," I told Eric one day. "I hope God will use me to reach out to women with unplanned pregnancies." I didn't know how this would play out, but I was confident God had put this burden on my heart for a reason.

On Labor Day weekend, our pastor dedicated Elizabeth at church, praying that God would watch over her all through her life and equip me and Eric to raise her. "Elizabeth means 'promise of God,'" he said as we stood before our friends. "There is a story in the Bible about a man named Nehemiah. He worked for the king and asked the king for permission to rebuild the city of Jerusalem, which had been destroyed. He then set out on a nearly impossible mission to rebuild the walls of Jerusalem and restore what was once there. Like Nehemiah, I believe your daughter will be a rebuilder and mend many relationships throughout her life."

Tears sprang to my eyes at his words. Despite our trials, Eric and my relationship had come full circle. Our business was now thriving, God had blessed us with a beautiful family and we'd found a wonderful church full of authentic people. I could only attribute all of this to God. As I'd watched our building burn to the ground that terrible December night, I'd been convinced our life was over. And as I'd watched my marriage crumble, I'd been convinced our once-fiery romance was nothing but smoldering ashes. But through the smoke came clear skies and with them, the promise of hope.

We'd made it through the fire. With God as our help, our marriage is great, and our love burns stronger.

IN A FOXHOLE
The Story of Michael
Written by Daniel Pouesi

The warning came only a few seconds before another rocket whizzed past our tent and detonated in a curtain of fire and smoke behind us. "Get down!"

The wooden frame and canvas walls of our tent shuddered on impact. The 5-foot walls of dirt-filled baskets on the sides barely absorbed the shock of the firestorm.

Heat seeped into our makeshift office. *This is it! We're all going to die.*

There was no way we were getting out. Even if we ran, we had nowhere to hide. Out in the open and miles from the nearest city, we were completely exposed to enemy fire.

The first mortar had descended like a preying beast. I reacted instinctively, screamed for my buddies to hit the ground, dropped to the floor myself and compacted into a ball.

The mortars kept up their death knell for about 10 minutes. They were the longest 10 minutes of my life. When I thought our situation couldn't get any worse, a blast shattered our door and ripped a hole the size of a Humvee in what used to be our front wall. The roof imploded and rained down shrapnel.

A dull ringing resonated in my head, and I felt sure

that the explosion had ruptured my eardrums. I tried to breathe, but dust and sand filled my nostrils. When I glanced up, I saw a wall of smoke develop before my eyes.

They say that the dead experience an out-of-body sensation the moment they die. Their lives flash before their eyes. Staring death in the eye, I thought of my wife and family. I had initially joined the Army to get away from my mother and stepfather. Now, I wondered what in the world I was doing in the war-ravaged, harsh dunes of a nation whose people considered America the Great Satan.

෩෩෩

I was born and raised in the city of Cagayan de Oro on the north coast of Mindanao, Philippines. Here, poverty revealed itself in the bloated stomachs and sunken eyes of many children. A travel writer described the city as "… unimpressive, a noisy mish-mash of busy streets and fast-food restaurants, hardly enough to tempt you to stay longer than a day or night before moving on to greener pastures." That was good advice for a tourist. But if you were born in Cagayan de Oro, you couldn't just book a flight and hop over to the next city to escape the poverty.

My grandmother raised me on a coconut farm on top of a swamp. My mother had moved into the city to work for the government — which was why she left me with my grandmother and cousins. Neglected and riddled with filthy puddles, our neighborhood was a favorite haunt for terrorists. People got robbed and sometimes killed in broad daylight. In spite of the crime and poverty, we made the best of what we had.

I lived in Cagayan de Oro until 1989 when my mother announced that she was marrying her pen pal, a Canadian named Allan Roberts. I didn't know what to make of her announcement, and I knew nothing about her boyfriend until the day he flew to the Philippines.

My cousins had done a thorough job of brainwashing me with horror stories of evil white men who ate little brown boys for dinner. It didn't help when a 6-foot giant with a full-grown beard walked into our home and my grandmother brought me out of the room to meet him. When he took my hand, I thought for sure I was a goner. I broke loose from his grip and ran screaming for the nearest room.

The next thing I knew, we were on a plane to Calgary, Canada.

When we landed, the cold bit my face and hands, and I pulled my shoulders together to keep warm. Smoke curled from my lips and startled me. I was 9. I thought for sure I was on fire.

In Calgary, everything was different. Even the people dressed, ate, sat and spoke differently. Suddenly in the midst of an English-speaking crowd, I couldn't recall a single English word I had learned in school. I tried to sift through all the new sensations and sounds, but when a lady stuck my arm with needles to inoculate me, it compounded a feeling of isolation.

A week later, my stepfather enrolled me in an ESL

class. Fully immersed in a new culture, I felt completely lost. At home, that sense of isolation intensified when my mother suddenly dropped our native language and adopted English. The transition was easy enough for her because she had worked in the Philippines as an assistant for the government where English was the primary language. In adopting English, she became even more of a stranger than she was when we were in the Philippines. I began to wonder if things would have been better for her and her new husband had I stayed in the Philippines. She didn't have to worry about me then. And I didn't need her to be home. Life in Cagayan de Oro was hard and unforgiving, but there was always someone — my grandmother or cousins — with whom I could talk, laugh and share experiences. Now I was alone, cut off from the only world I knew.

Six months after we landed in Canada, I couldn't deal with the isolation anymore. Sitting at the dining table one evening, the tears came unbidden. Surrounded by the amenities of a good life and living without fear of terrorists or thieves, I found myself wishing I was in a plane headed back home.

"What's wrong with you?" my mother asked.

"I want to go back to Cagayan de Oro," I replied.

"That's the thanks I get for taking you out of that filth." She stalked out of the room.

෧෧෧

IN A FOXHOLE

Life in our new home was a huge step up from our swamp in the Philippines. A diesel and airplane mechanic, my stepfather owned a big home and earned a decent living. He did some of his work at home. He tolerated my presence as long as I didn't get in his way. I hung out around the garage while he worked on his engines. Seldom did a word pass between us. Meanwhile, my mother found a job as a nanny in a wealthy neighborhood. In her interaction with people, she found friends and went out with them to parties. As in the Philippines, I was pretty much left to my own devices.

One of the things that magnified my feeling of solitude was the constant moves. Just when I was settling in and making new friends, it was time to move again. We lived in Calgary for about a year and a half, then moved to Airdrie, the next city over, to be close to my stepfather's business. The same year, my sister, Christine, was born.

We lived in Airdrie for a few years, then my stepfather found a reason to move again. He complained about the high taxes and how much he disliked living among the French. Although Canada is considered one of the wealthiest countries in the world, his heart was set on relocating to the United States. He sold his business, purchased a home trailer and moved us to a trailer park in Las Vegas, Nevada.

Though we were better off than some of our neighbors, our possessions masked a deeper problem. We hardly spoke. Under the same roof, we existed in our own separate worlds. I understood why my mother and stepfather were together. They needed each other. But what was my purpose? Did I mean anything to them? Or was I an inconvenience? Because there was little love and affection in our family, I assumed I was the cause.

Essentially my mother and stepfather became like mirrors. I saw reflected in their words and actions who I was. In their silence, I saw myself as a nonperson. When they didn't say a word of praise or thank me for something I did, I told myself something was wrong with me. Because nothing I did seemed to please them, I was convinced I was incapable of doing anything right. Everything I attempted, I came up short in their eyes — or mine. I could wash and dry the dishes, but there was always a plate that wasn't thoroughly cleaned or dried or put away right. I may bring home a passing grade but, in my mind, it wasn't good enough. I didn't deserve their love and acceptance.

My mother and stepfather didn't physically abuse me. But the body language and their silence cut to the heart. I masked and buried the hurt and told myself that if I worked just a bit harder, they would come around and see me differently.

One evening, I decided to make them dinner. I got out the rice cooker and made rice. Then I prepared a special chicken dish. In the evening, when my mother returned from work, I had the table all set. She took one look at it and said, "What's all this?"

"It's chicken and rice," I replied.

She furrowed her brow and said, "Take it away!"

She grabbed the bowl of chicken and emptied it in the trash. She did the same with the rice, then marched out of the room complaining about how wasteful my effort had been. I watched her disappear into the next room, my body racked with a slew of emotions. Misery descended like quicksand over me, and I grabbed a knife off the table and pressed it to my stomach. A stray thought kept my hand at bay. *If I kill myself, who would take care of my sister?* Shaking off my depression, I flung the knife on the floor and went to church. I needed to be around other people. I needed some assurance that there was a reason for my existence.

At the youth group meeting that night, the youth pastor, Peter, must have sensed trouble, for he came and sat beside me.

"How are you, Michael?"

"Not too good."

"What's going on?"

All the bottled-up emotions burst forth. Occasionally, Peter acknowledged with a nod. When I said that I was nothing, he wrapped an arm around my shoulder and said, "Michael, you're somebody. And I want to show that to you, if you'll let me."

I didn't say a word, so he continued. "Do you think you're here by accident?"

"I feel that way sometimes, like I wasn't meant to be born."

"You feel that way because you think your mother doesn't care about you. I can't speak for your mother because I don't know what she's going through. The only person who knows is God. So let's talk about you."

Peter took a pocket-sized Bible and parted it in the middle. He found a verse and said, "This is what a man who understood rejection wrote. 'Though my father and mother forsake me, the Lord will receive me.' Michael, you're not a nobody. You're someone in God's eyes. He created you in his image. Do you know what that means? He has a plan and purpose for you. You're not an accident."

He flipped to the back section of the Bible and found another verse. "Here's what another man named Paul said. Paul also knew how it was to be rejected, abandoned by friends and his own people. He said in Ephesians 2:10, 'For we are God's workmanship, created in Christ Jesus to do good works, which God prepared in advance for us to do.'"

Peter closed the Bible, then added, "The word 'workmanship' comes from the Greek 'poiema,' meaning poem or masterpiece. That means we are God's poem. We are his masterpiece. If that doesn't make anyone feel special, then I don't know what will. That verse also tells me that we were made to have a relationship with God. A relationship with him is the only way we can satisfy the deep desires of our heart; that includes the desire to receive and give love. Someone once said that God made us for himself, and our hearts are restless until we find that rest in him. Michael, would you like to know how you can have that relationship with God?"

I hesitated. Why would anyone accept a bad person like me? I'd heard of God's acceptance of people, but my warped sense of self gave me the impression that God's acceptance was only for good people. If I couldn't cut mustard with my mother and stepfather, how could I with a perfect God?

"We'll never be good enough to buy God's love," Peter said. "His acceptance is based on the fact that his son, Jesus, died to make us right with him. All God is asking is that we believe in his son."

That night, Peter introduced me to Jesus. I asked for forgiveness for the bad things I did and especially for attempting to take my life. Following Pastor Peter's lead, I asked Jesus to come into my heart. Before I left, Peter said, "Michael, this doesn't mean everything is going to be perfect at home or elsewhere from now on. We will still face problems because we live in a broken world. But having a relationship with God means he'll be there to help. I'm here for you, too."

My problems didn't disappear, just as Peter said. In fact, some things got worse, and I found myself riddled with even deeper feelings of self-doubt and low self-esteem. At home, life became so demoralizing that I stayed away after school. I joined the school band. And at one time, I even considered joining a gang.

Things at school weren't much better.

One morning, my homeroom teacher motioned me to his desk. Standing beside him, arms crossed, was a student named Stanley. He came from a well-to-do family.

"Stanley tells me that you stole his watch," the teacher said.

Having just warded off a round of criticism at home, I felt as though the teacher had planted his heel on my solar plexus. I stared at Stanley. "Why did you say that?"

"You're a thief," Stanley replied, looking at the teacher for support.

"What do you have to say for yourself?" the teacher asked me.

I stood there aghast, confused, wondering what people saw in me that they could so easily accuse me of wrongdoing without an offer of proof.

Unable to defend myself against this new barrage of accusations, I simply said, "I did not steal his watch." I turned to leave, but the teacher caught my arm.

He studied me then, apparently convinced that he wasn't going to get a confession, and ordered me back to my seat. "I'll take this up with the principal."

That brought little comfort. What chance did I have against a kid who had everything and no reason to lie?

The next day while I pored over a book in reading class, the classroom door opened, and a couple of policemen entered. They spoke with the teacher, and she pointed in my direction.

One of the two officers walked up to me and told me to stand. In front of everyone, he cuffed me, read me my rights, then led me away to the principal's office. They questioned me about Stanley's watch, and I told them I didn't take it.

"Tell the truth — or the officers will take you away," the principal said.

"I didn't steal the watch," I repeated. I resigned myself to the belief that nothing I said mattered. There was something really wrong with me.

After a brief conference with the principal, the arresting officer took me back to class, released me at the door and told me to join the other students. The classroom went suddenly quiet when I entered and walked down the aisle to my desk. I felt nothing. Moments later, when some of the boys said how cool it was to be handcuffed by the police, I felt strangely odd. The only real praise I received was not for doing good but for getting in trouble with the police.

Shortly after, my mother opened a summons for me to appear in court. She went into her diatribe, calling me a loser, an embarrassment. She refused to accompany me to the court, and so my stepfather reluctantly assigned himself the shameful task. At the court, a public defender counseled me to plead guilty. My stepfather agreed. A feeling of betrayal coursed through my veins. How could I defend myself when even those closest to me didn't give me the benefit of the doubt? Mulling over the consequences of a guilty plea, I was tempted to go along just to spite my mother. But I shook my head and said no.

My stepfather turned a shade lighter. "Why not?"

"Because I didn't steal the watch."

"You will do as you're told."

"No," I repeated and threatened to walk out.

Fortunately for everyone, the judge ruled in my favor after he found out the officers had cuffed and interrogated me without notifying my parents.

❧❧❧

After the stolen watch incident, the rift in our family widened. I went to a church called Calvary Four Square for no other reason than to get away. It was around this time that we moved from the trailer park. My stepfather bought a piece of property on the west side of Las Vegas and built a house. Because he was no longer employed, my mother hired herself out as a cashier in a casino to support our family. Though her absence deepened the silence at home, it brought some relief; I did not have to listen to her criticism.

I joined the ROTC program in high school and made up my mind to join the Army at 17. I couldn't wait to get out. My mother refused to sign the release form. But two months after graduation, I took the placement test without her knowledge, and the recruiter offered me two choices. "You can either be a cook or join the infantry."

Cook seemed a safe choice, but the word that came out of my mouth was "Infantry." I had this fatalistic attitude toward myself — if I die, so be it. I had lost sight of my talk with Pastor Peter about God's purpose for my life.

Not surprisingly, my mother lambasted my decision. I wanted out. I wanted to do my own thing without her or my stepfather criticizing or belittling me.

When I left for boot camp in Georgia, she and my stepfather didn't see me off. And they didn't attend my graduation. After my graduation ceremony, I did call home to tell them I was coming for a two-week break. They weren't at the airport to pick me up. I caught a shuttle to a friend's home.

Because I didn't receive love, I found it very difficult to give it.

ॐॐॐ

That attitude changed almost overnight when Amy walked into my life. I met her in Germany during a deployment. A Cambodian-American, she served as a combat medic in the Army.

We dated, and as our relationship blossomed, I felt a connection with her that I had never experienced with my mother. Suddenly, I mattered. Amy exuded love and care and showed genuine interest in me and my dreams, though I really didn't have any. Despite the fact I had accomplished something, I still felt like a jetsam out on the high seas. Our friendship developed, and we found ourselves falling in love. One day, I asked for her hand in marriage.

We exchanged vows in her hometown, San Diego, before a justice of the peace. Amy's parents were present, and so was my sister. I didn't feel like calling my mother or stepfather, though I suspected that they knew of my special day.

BEAUTIFULLY WRECKED

❧❧❧

My first deployment was to Kosovo. We flew out at the heels of the so-called Kosovo Conflict. Kosovo is a region in Southeastern Europe. The majority of its population was ethnic Albanians. The region was largely autonomous until Serbian leader Milosevic brought it under control of the Serbian capital, Belgrade. The Kosovar Albanians protested. Unrest in the region escalated and led to open conflict between the Serbian police and the Kosovar Albanians that displaced thousands of people.

There were a lot of conflicting stories about the United States' and President Bill Clinton's involvement in the conflict. Some accused the president of purposely engaging U.S. troops to distract citizens from his scandalous affair with White House intern, Monica Lewinsky. As soldiers, we weren't supposed to question our Commander in Chief. We simply followed orders.

When we took a bus from Macedonia to Kosovo, we had our fingers on our triggers because we didn't know what to expect. We didn't engage in combat, but we watched Albanians fight from hilltops.

We were stationed in Camp Monteith, a military base near a place called Gnjilane. The camp initially consisted of one main building, which served as a command post, and a few small outbuildings. It also had a number of semi-permanent barracks called Seahuts. Our mission was to patrol the borders of Kosovo and Albania and provide police security. We were allowed to interact with locals.

They didn't have much — most of their shelters resembled mud huts set in woodland areas with clusters of greenery. In winter, the snow dressed up the foliage and rooftops in postcard-like sceneries. The town itself had a European old town feel to it; it was broken down in places.

The deployment was only for six months, but time seemed to stretch forever. Then on September 11, 2001, Muslim terrorists on a suicide mission hijacked and crashed American commercial airplanes into the Twin Towers of the World Trade Center in New York City, and everything changed. George Walker Bush had been named the 43rd President of the United States. On that day, friends and I were in the office doing paperwork when we got word that an airplane had crashed into the North Tower of the World Trade Center in New York. We turned on our television and watched with disbelief as a second airplane, United Flight 175, plowed into the South Tower. The base immediately went into a lockdown. Our superiors pumped up security, and we hauled out our combat gear into the camp in preparation for new orders.

The September 11 attack topped the news worldwide for the next few weeks. Much of the time, we wore full battle gear and mourned the loss of American lives. I thought of what Pastor Peter said about God creating man to have a relationship with him and with others. If man were a product of blind evolution, then the loss of lives wouldn't have mattered. The fact that a nation and millions of people around the world lamented the death of innocent Americans convinced me it did. I thought of my family and realized how selfish and foolish I had been to think that my life didn't matter. The September attack not only destroyed lives but precious relationships. An official letter later explained who was behind the attack — the radical and militant Muslim Osama Bin Laden, who founded the jihadist Islamic organization, Al-Qaeda.

In a stirring speech to the nation, President Bush vowed to go after the perpetrators and included among them any country that harbored them. With talk of war brewing, I prayed that I would have time to go home to be with my family.

In March 2003, the United States attacked Iraq.

Home on furlough, I knew we were headed for Iraq. A sudden dread started to gnaw at my faith. Then came a profound sense of sadness. Amy was about to give birth to our firstborn, and I wanted more than anything to be with her. The Army wouldn't extend my stay. But after rethinking my situation, my superior granted me an additional four months. Time never tasted so sweet or felt more precious than when he said that I could stay with Amy a bit longer. With the deployment looming over me, I suddenly had a reason to live. I wanted to be with my wife and see our son grow up. But duty also called.

My platoon and I flew to Kuwait and stayed there for two weeks, then deployed to Iraq. The initial air campaign had died down. Driving through the south, we saw blown-out buildings and vehicles piled one on top of each other in crumbled heaps. The devastation was mind-boggling. It looked like an "Invasion from Outer Space" movie set. From our camp at St. Michael, we headed north to Baghdad and witnessed more destruction. Behind every single one of them, I saw shattered lives and relationships: A child struggled with the loss of a parent, or a father mourned the death of his entire family. The mere vision of them sent a flash of grief rippling throughout my body. When I joined the military, I just wanted out of my mother's presence. With a family of my own, family relationships suddenly meant something to me. I prayed for protection for my family, my friends and me. We slept with our protective gear on, nerves on fire. We celebrated when our deployment was about to end. Counting the days, we packed our bags, ready at a moment's notice to fly out. Then we got orders that our deployment had been extended three more months. It had already been a long year, and the new orders drew complaints. The search for Saddam Hussein was in full swing. We had no choice but to hunker down.

It was then that the rockets hit us. They came out of nowhere, inflicting swift destruction and bellowing out their deadly, thunderous song. There was nothing any one of us could do but hug the floor and wait them out. Never in my life had I called on God's name more furiously or more earnestly than I did those 10 enduring minutes while mortars and rockets rained down around us.

Please, God, I want to see my family again.

࿔࿔࿔

My relationship with God grew after that initial Iraq experience. One might say that it was just luck that saved me. But I know better. Luck couldn't give the kind of peace I experienced under attack. And luck couldn't have given me the confidence to bear up under intense pressure.

My belief in God didn't instantly eliminate fear. For me, faith in God came gradually. Following a yearlong break, I returned to Iraq. This time, my wife was pregnant with our second child. The timing couldn't have been worse, but in an unusual show of grace, my mother took leave from work and volunteered to help Amy. Things weren't working out for her and my stepfather. At the time, I selfishly felt that it wasn't my problem. I had enough of my own.

One day, while stationed at the FOB (Forward Operating Base) in Askandria, Iraq, we got word that one of our vehicles had been hit by a bomb. Some of our soldiers were seriously hurt. We climbed into our Humvees and drove out to help.

In training, we were taught to stay alert for dirt mounds on the roads. They could be signs of planted explosives.

I remember swerving to the left, and the next thing I knew, everything turned dark. Dust swirled all around. The vehicle stopped moving. Then on its own, it steered back to the right and rolled into a ditch. All of our panel equipment shut down as if a hand had reached in and severed the power.

"Why did you stop?" my friend on the passenger side asked.

"I didn't," I replied. "It stopped by itself."

My friend looked down and started screaming. Shrapnel had penetrated the Humvee's underbelly and pierced his legs. My gunner, who sat behind us, leaned forward, and I noticed that gunpowder had burned his neck and part of his face. When I veered to the left, I had triggered a pressure plate improvised explosive device. We crawled out. The blast had separated the Humvee's hood and totaled its front end. The force blew out the tires on the passenger side and fractured the windows.

Amazingly, I didn't have a single scratch on me.

Someone speculated that either the bomb was defective or whoever planted it buried it too deeply, otherwise it would have blown up the Humvee. I had my own theory. God placed a shield over us and saved us from certain death.

Still shaken from the experience, I watched my friends return to camp before joining the rest of the team to complete our mission.

෨෨෨෨

The war experience changed my outlook on life. I saw a reason for living and enjoying time with friends and family. After my first deployment, my mom became more of a mother. For the first time, she expressed her pride in me. She sent letters and care packages. Unfortunately, while things were shaping up for Amy and me, they were going downhill for her and my stepfather. I tried to encourage her. During my third deployment, they divorced.

I returned home via March Air Force Base in Riverside, California. My wife and sons came to meet me. A fire truck hosed down our aircraft in a symbolic gesture. Refreshed and filled with hope, I disembarked with my buddies. I embraced the ground, then hugged my wife and kids as a crowd cheered and waved flags and banners. I waved back over Amy's shoulder, and as my gaze flitted from one person to the next, I caught sight of my mother standing among strangers, her fingers interlaced under her chin. When our eyes met, her lips parted in a big smile. Slowly, she unclasped her hands and wagged a forefinger at me. That playful gesture said more to me about her pride than words could express. I savored the moment, telling myself that I couldn't have asked for a better "Welcome Back Home" gift. I fought back tears and thanked God for bringing me safely to my family. As my wife, our two boys and I followed the rest of the soldiers to the airport lounge, I recited in silence a passage from the Bible that gave me hope.

> The LORD is my light and my salvation —
> so why should I be afraid?
> The LORD is my fortress, protecting me from danger,
> so why should I tremble?
> When evil people come to devour me,
> when my enemies and foes attack me,

they will stumble and fall.
Though a mighty army surrounds me,
my heart will not be afraid.
Even if I am attacked,
I will remain confident.
(Psalm 27:1-3 NLT)

I can't explain why, but I believe that the verses were a personal message to me from God. They reminded me that I had a purpose and that God would see me through it. I knew soldiers who were afraid to go out or do their jobs when things got intense. My faith gave me the confidence to follow through. My faith in a God who has control of every aspect of my life gave me a boldness that the world can't give. In hindsight, my deployments were an opportunity to exercise that faith.

As we walked from the lounge to our car, I squeezed my mother's shoulder and gave her an encouraging smile. "Mom, I'm so sorry about the divorce. Is there anything I can do for you?"

She hesitated, my firstborn cuddled in her arms. Then a smile formed at the corners of her mouth, and tears brimmed her eyes and slid down her cheek. "Nothing," she replied, planting a kiss on my son's check. "I have everything."

"I love you, Mom," I said and opened the car door for her and full entrance into my heart.

FIFTH AND BROADWAY
The Story of Marie
Written by Rebekah Henwood

The sound of my children's laughter filled the warm June air as we passed neighborhood kids playing basketball. I waved at a neighbor walking his dog, feeling happy and thinking how lucky I was to live in such a great community. Our kids talked energetically about the great meal we just shared as a family as my husband, Daniel, pulled his Dodge Ram truck into the driveway. The smell of neighbors cooking dinner intermingled with the fragrance of pine, which was a rare scent in San Diego, but common to our neighborhood.

The screaming sound of a car barreling down our street pierced the lighthearted mood as our kids jumped out of the truck and we headed to the front door. I turned and watched Dad's fancy $100,000 Mercedes Benz tear into the driveway, the door flying open as it came to a screeching halt. With his neck veins protruding more than usual and hazel eyes stormy with rage, Dad jumped out of the car and ran toward us.

He jumped in front of Daniel, right in his face. "You motherf*****!"

"Get the kids in the house!" I said to my mother-in-law who was visiting from out of town. She had heard stories of my dad's rage, but this would be her first personal experience. "Shut the door! Lock it! Keep the kids inside!"

"How dare you talk to my husband this way!" I tried to wedge myself in between my dad's large 6-foot, 3-inch body and Daniel.

"This isn't about you, Marie, this is about your husband!" His piercing eyes flashed back to Daniel. "You're a loser, Daniel. You are a horrible provider. Marie married a loser! Look at how well her sisters have married. She should have married someone who would take care of her." Dad stuck his finger right in Daniel's face, his flashy gold Rolex shaking as he tossed his finger back and forth.

"You're a piece of trash! My grandchildren deserve so much better than you! You don't have a job. You haven't bought a house yet!"

I could see the restraint in Daniel's calm blue eyes. Dad was pushing my sweet, kindhearted husband's buttons — a very difficult thing to do. I saw Daniel's fists tighten as he stood there, stoically, allowing Dad to scream and belittle him.

I kept trying to get between them. "Get the h*** out of here, Dad! I'm going to call the police!"

"You need to move out; you can't live here anymore!" Dad snapped back. "You owe me money! You have no idea what's coming to you." He stomped back to his car.

My heart was pounding out of my chest. I hadn't witnessed an angry explosion like this in a while, but it was definitely a familiar scene.

It took me right back to the rage-filled moments of my childhood.

FIFTH AND BROADWAY

෯෯෯

When I was 16, we lived way out in the country. My friends and I didn't have driver's licenses yet, but my friends would often drive to and from each other's homes on back roads. Their parents didn't care.

Maegan had been over for the afternoon but had to get home or she would be in big trouble. My parents weren't home, so I jumped in my dad's small green Toyota pickup truck and made the 10-minute roundtrip to drop Maegan off. As I pulled up to my house, I looked in the rearview mirror to see my dad coming up the driveway.

Before I could even get out, Dad flung my door open, pulled me out by my hair, threw me on the ground and kicked me.

Dad picked me up and started shaking me. "Where the f*** have you been?"

"Dad, I was giving her …"

"Don't f****** talk to me. Get in your room! You're such a f****** whore!" His eyes were filled with rage.

I ran to my room. Dad chased after me, whipping off his leather belt from around his waist — something he did quite often. I managed to get in my room and lock the door. He banged on the door, over and over, then finally disappeared. I picked up the phone to call for help, but he had already disconnected the line.

He came back to the door, this time using a screwdriver or some kind of tool to open the door.

"You have no business taking my car! What do you

think you are doing?" He smacked me across the face. "You're such a pain in my a**! Out of all my kids, you're the one! You're the one!"

❧❧❧

I had a feeling something wasn't right with my family. My 9-year-old intuition was strong. Something was definitely up.

Grandpa, Mom's dad, came to visit us from New York City. Grandpa was so cool. He was an artist, an atheist and always read the newspaper and big books — a true intellectual. I loved climbing up in his lap as he sipped his coffee through his big grey beard. My family was from the Church of Latter Day Saints (LDS), or Mormons, so we never had coffee in our house. But I loved the smell. I was drawn to Grandpa. He was so different than most of the people in my life, and I was captivated by his differences.

Our house had a wooden custom-built phone "booth" under the stairs. Inside the booth was a cozy private area with a stool and phone. The wood door had frosted glass panels etched with "Phone 5 cents." It made a great hiding place during games of hide-n-seek.

I peeked into the door to see Dad and Grandpa crowded around the phone, listening to someone's conversation. They saw me and quickly waved me away.

Who were they listening to? Listening to someone's phone conversation was completely unheard of in this house! What was going on?

I briskly checked all the phones in the house and found my mother talking to someone on the phone in her bedroom. They were listening to Mom!

A strange feeling caused my heart to sink. *I think Dad is going to leave ... and never come back.*

A few days later, I ran down the road to the Lees' house. We met the Lees a few years prior when my parents built our beautiful, fancy home in an upscale neighborhood in Northern California. This home was like a fairytale. We lived in a strong LDS community and were very active in the Mormon church.

The Lees were like family to us. They had six children, five of whom were the same ages as me and my four siblings. We attended the same school and church and spent vacations together in Yosemite and Lake Tahoe. Our home was their home and vice versa. Our doors were always open. We never knocked, we just let ourselves in.

This day was different. I tried to open the door at the Lees' house and was surprised to find it locked. I knocked on the door, and Sister Lee answered.

"Marie, you can't play here anymore. You aren't welcome here." Her words were curt, with an unfamiliar tone.

"Why? I just want to play with the girls!" I didn't understand.

"I don't want you to ever come back here again. You go ask your mom why. She can tell you."

I was so confused. *After all the years of wonderful friendship, I just don't get it.*

I was really angry at Mom. *What did she do?* Of course, I could never really ask her. Children were to be seen and not heard.

There were certain unwritten codes of family life in the LDS community. When I was baptized in the Church of Latter Day Saints, I had so many questions. I didn't feel right about the baptism. But I couldn't ask my questions, and I couldn't get any answers because that just isn't how things work. I did as I was told.

I started hearing rumors about my family, about my mom. People were talking about us in an unfavorable light. Turned out, my mother had an extensive affair with Brother Lee, a man high up in the LDS church, whose family had been our best friends for years. *How could this be happening?*

One day, my older siblings, Elisabeth and Sam, walked out of my parents' bedroom after some kind of meeting. Elisabeth's eyes were bright red and swollen from crying. She was sobbing so hard she was hiccupping. Sam's face was stone cold, expressionless.

Mom and Dad said they were calling a family meeting. Normally, this was a good thing. Normally, they would announce we were going to Disneyland or doing something fun as a family. But I could tell this time the news wasn't good.

Mom and Dad called us into the formal living room, a tell-tale sign of the seriousness of this meeting. Traditionally, the formal living room was off limits to us children, except to play the piano. Elisabeth sat in a far corner of the room, removed from the rest of the family, hugging her knees in despair. Mom held little David in her lap, as she kept her eyes downcast. I sat on the couch with Chloe and an expressionless Sam, anticipating the news. Kneeling on the floor, as he always does for any family meeting or important announcement, Dad told us he would be moving out for a while. An abnormal silence suddenly filled the room.

"Everything will be fine. We aren't getting divorced." I wasn't buying their attempt at reassuring us. No one in the LDS church gets divorced. Ever! But I knew my parents were full of it. This was it. My little 9-year-old heart was broken.

Our strong Mormon community quickly unraveled. We weren't welcome anymore — not at church, not at people's homes. We were the black sheep. People were mean to us, constantly talking about us behind our backs.

Mom and Dad got divorced and sold the beautiful fairytale house. I was devastated, angry and distant from everyone. It seemed to affect me much more than my siblings.

Why is this so much harder for me than everyone else? Why was I born into this family? Everyone hates us. There is no love anywhere. This must be what God is like — one mistake and we are abandoned.

I had even more questions now.

࿔࿔࿔

Dad pulled up to Mom's tiny house one summer morning to take Chloe, David and me to the beach for a picnic. He was driving a white BMW. I had never met anyone who drove a BMW. We got in the car, and I immediately noticed the cute blond curly-haired little boy with dimples in his cheeks, sitting in the back seat. He was about the same age as David. In the front was a woman I had never met. She was very beautiful, with long curly hair.

As we drove off, I heard an unfamiliar sound on the radio. *Is that ROCK music?* I had never listened to rock music before.

"Who's singing?"

"Pink Floyd," Debbie responded with a smile.

This lady is wild! We are in a BMW listening to rock music! When we got to the beach, she got even wilder. As we stripped down to our swimsuits, Debbie took off her clothes to reveal a tiny purple strapless top with a ring in the center. I had never seen anyone wear a bikini before! The skimpy bottoms were pieced together by a ring on either hip.

She is so cool! She is definitely not a Mormon. I had never met a woman like her. She was loud, and she had an opinion. And she even said a few cuss words.

I knocked on Dad's bedroom door one morning after I spent the night.

"Just a minute! Just a minute! Hold on!" I heard shuffling feet and something being thrown around. Dad finally came to the door. Just behind him on the floor, I saw a makeshift "bed" of sheets and blankets. Debbie was in my dad's bed wearing a beautiful skimpy nightgown. I had never seen a nightgown like that.

They are sleeping together! I couldn't believe it. This was completely forbidden and unheard of in the LDS church.

My dad's infidelity really bugged me, but Debbie was very nice to us. She took my sisters and me to get our hair done. She took us to the nail salon for us to get fake fingernails. She even gave me her Macy's charge card so I could go shopping.

Once Dad and Debbie announced their engagement, I didn't like her so much. I planned to show my disapproval at the wedding when the minister asked if anyone had any objections. I was going to stand up, and I was going to speak out my disapproval! Of course, I didn't do that. I kept quiet.

As one of the bridesmaids, I was required to wear an awful long, strapless fuchsia dress. It was hideous. To make matters worse, when I put the dress on, it didn't fit me, despite having been sized and altered. I had to stuff tissue in the bust to hold it up. I blamed this on Debbie. *She did this on purpose! Elisabeth looks beautiful, but I look awful!*

Despite my anger, I eventually moved in with Dad and Debbie. They built a beautiful house on the 6-acre lot my parents purchased when they were still married. The idea of having my own room and a brand-new house was too appealing to pass up.

❧❧❧

My first real interaction with Daniel occurred during my sophomore year as I was walking down the hall of our high school in between periods. Daniel was a senior and the typical guy every girl wanted to date. He was the star of the football team, homecoming king and, of course, very handsome.

He was standing against a locker with his football buddies as I walked toward him, alone, on my way to gym class. I felt intimidated as I approached his group. He and his friends seemed so cool and popular, and I was just a nobody.

"Check her out, man, she has a nice body!" One of his buddies nudged him as Daniel flashed me a smile. "Yeah, she is pretty! Go for it, Daniel!"

I was flattered — I couldn't believe these cool guys thought I was attractive.

After school that day, Daniel offered me a ride home in his cool Toyota truck. I accepted, and we began dating. I later found out Daniel told his friends to stop talking about his "future wife."

Turned out, Daniel's circle of friends was known as a group of partying druggies. Now that Daniel and I were dating, rumors started surfacing about me doing drugs. I had never touched drugs, but I eventually gave up defending myself and just didn't care what anyone thought. All I cared about was Daniel and the attention he gave me.

Daniel had witnessed the dysfunction of my family and the rage and abuse of my dad and promised to one day rescue me from my family life. I wasn't completely convinced he would fulfill that promise, but he showed me love and comfort I had never seen from my father. I was secure in our relationship.

During my senior year, Daniel drove me home to my dad's house after school. I walked up to the porch to find all of my belongings piled up with a note from Dad. "You are no longer welcome to live here." He had changed the locks, and I couldn't get inside.

My grandfather on my dad's side wrote a book about his great-grandfather who was a bodyguard for Brigham Young, one of the founders of the LDS church. Grandfather wrote the book with the intention of making it into a Hollywood movie.

It was filled with all kinds of family secrets — a murder my great-grandfather committed, physical abuse my grandfather suffered and more. My dad forbade me to read the book; he didn't want me asking questions about our family's past. But I had questions, so I read the book. My dad had discovered I was reading it and flew into another one of his rages.

Now it was my turn to fly into a rage. I threw everything on that porch all over the yard. I scattered my clothes everywhere. I took a 3-foot-tall clay cactus and bashed it with my hands, over and over and over.

My anger at Dad seeped into other aspects of life. I built up a wall around me, prohibiting new relationships from forming and virtually extinguishing those that already existed. I didn't trust anyone.

After taking an "I don't care" approach and barely graduating from high school, Dad reached out to me and asked me to go to counseling with him. He was finally seeing someone about his rage issues. I loved seeing the counselor; I loved being able to talk to someone and have someone listen.

After Dad reached out to me, I started back to work at one of the health food stores he owned in Northern California. The health food stores always attracted different types of people than I was used to. I was intrigued by the various New Agers and free thinkers. They were different; I was drawn to different.

Ruth was an older lady who worked with me at the store. Her short salt-and-pepper hair, glasses and crystal jewelry gave her a mystical appearance, which intrigued me. I gravitated toward her. She was my mentor, a pseudo-grandmother of sorts.

"Marie, you have such a strong intuition." She told me this frequently. "You really need to learn to channel that intuition."

Ruth was a master teacher of Reiki, a spiritual healing energy bodywork. Ruth asked me to be one of her students. I felt so honored that a master Reiki teacher would ask me to be a student; I jumped at the opportunity and even got certified to practice Reiki.

Searching for something, I knew I wasn't going back to the Mormon faith. I had been to the Southern Baptist church where Daniel's dad preached, and that was definitely not for me. I wanted something spiritual, something New Age and something with crystals and astrology.

I learned about Wicca from a friend at the store who was a witch and started using tarot cards; I was even paid to read astrology charts.

Ruth gave me a beautiful statue of a goddess. We built an altar for her, lit candles and Ruth taught me how to pray to her. I loved it! I felt such a strong connection to something, finally. *This is true religion. This is it. This is what I have been searching for.*

֎֎֎

I was setting up the produce display in one of my dad's health food stores. My growing belly was making this job quite tasking. I had yet to feel Rose move inside of me and was starting to feel nervous.

Paul was a sweet older man who worked alongside me at the store. He genuinely cared for me. His baby blue eyes were warm and welcoming, and you could see through them to the kindness of his heart. With his grey hair and mustache, along with the upright way in which he carried himself, he seemed like a prophet.

While Daniel's parents and my mom continually pressured us to get married, and my dad and stepmom seemed to roll their eyes at me, Paul always assured me it was okay. His support was a welcome change. I was not going to marry Daniel. I was going to be a single mom and raise this baby by myself, because that is what women do these days.

"Paul, I'm worried because I haven't felt Rose move yet. I'm starting to get nervous," I said, sharing my fear with him.

"Let me pray for you, Marie." I knew Paul was a Christian, but no one had ever prayed for me like that. "Dear God, I pray that you will keep baby Rose safe and send Marie a sign that her baby is okay. Please protect her. Amen."

It felt awesome to have Paul pray for me. I felt so loved. Right then, Rose kicked for the first time! Surely, this was the sign from God for which Paul prayed. It was the first time I had heard from God or seen evidence of his presence in my life. I never thought he cared, but perhaps I was wrong. *Maybe I should look more into this Christian thing.*

Before too long, Daniel and I began attending church with Paul. It was nearing Christmastime, and I was basking in the wonder of being pregnant so close to Christmas. I felt like Mary, mother of Jesus, whom I was learning more and more about in the Bible; yet I was still carrying around the guilt of being pregnant and unmarried. (Ironically, she was pregnant and not married to her betrothed, Joseph!)

One Sunday while at Paul's church, a week before Rose was born, I agreed to pray and asked Jesus to come into my life and be my Savior. It eased my fears and gave me more hope. But because my guilt-driven decision was not genuine, I quickly drifted back to my New Age friends with whom I felt a greater connection.

Not long after that, a customer at the health food store asked me if I had read *You Are Your Child's First Teacher.* It is a book about Waldorf education and raising your kids in a Waldorf home, where you pray to mother earth, father sun and give thanks to the grains. The Jesus decision definitely didn't stick.

The customer bought me a copy of the book, and I loved reading it. I connected with it and loved the idea. I felt so strongly about this that I enrolled in school to become a teacher of Waldorf education.

We were rarely going to church anymore, as my newfound spiritual experience of Waldorf education replaced church.

Being a Waldorf teacher was a perfect fit for my spiritual way of life. I felt it perfectly defined my philosophy on life. It felt like completion — my spiritual life was whole.

જ્જ્જ્જ

It was a chilly November morning in the mountains of Northern California. The smell of fresh bread rising on the hearth filled the room as the sounds of the fire crackling blended into the background. I was holding Jonas in my arms when the phone rang. It was Dad.

"Marie, your grandfather is dead. He killed himself."

My grandfather put a gun in his mouth and pulled the trigger just months after my uncle killed himself.

Remarkably, the news really didn't faze me. I didn't cry, I didn't drop to the floor with grief. I felt sadness for my grandmother who found him in a pool of blood. I felt sad for the eight children and 27 grandchildren he left behind. I felt bitter. I felt angry.

I contrasted my grandfather's suicide to the recent death of my sister's father-in-law. He lost his battle to cancer after desperately wanting to live, fighting to live, to be with his family. How could my grandfather just give up and be so selfish?

Dad flew all of us kids to Utah for the funeral. More than 30 of my cousins were there. I looked around at everyone crying on that chilly morning and felt angry. *This was his decision,* I thought bitterly. *He chose to end his life because the guilt and the secrets were too much for him to handle.* To me, Grandpa was a nasty man who acted very spiritual — a man who was respected for his high position in the LDS church. Even his death had to be disguised. He didn't commit suicide, he had "a heart attack." Mormons don't commit suicide.

This whole Mormon thing is definitely not for me. How could a "good" God allow someone to kill himself in his own house and leave behind his wife, children and grandchildren? No, I don't think God is good at all.

⇜⇜⇜

For five years, Daniel held a great position working in Dad's health food chain. One day, completely out of the blue, Dad fired Daniel.

Life had been perfect for us. Daniel and I had been married for about eight years, the kids were in a great school, I had a wonderful teaching job, which I loved, we had great health insurance and benefits and we loved where we lived. But that was all coming to an end.

Dad gave us an idea of moving to San Diego and living in one of the several homes he owned there. He made it all sound so appealing — we could live rent-free, take a few months to get our feet on the ground and just relax. It sounded like an extended vacation.

Within three weeks, I resigned from my teaching job, pulled the kids out of school, gave notice to our landlords and we moved our lives to San Diego. And it *was* like a vacation. We enrolled the kids in a great school 30 minutes from the house, and I got a job at a boutique in Gaslamp, the downtown party area, while I studied mixology so I could become a cocktail waitress.

Jonas received an invitation from a classmate to visit a local church called Canvas Church. We had never thought about going to church as a family — our days of attending with Paul had passed — but since the kids didn't have the spiritual environment they had at their school in Northern California, we decided it would be good for them to try a church.

The atmosphere at Canvas Church was completely different than I anticipated. To my surprise, the people wore hip, trendy clothes to the services — jeans, fashionable tops, cute shoes — things I would wear! This was a far cry from the stuffy suits, ties, dresses and tights I was accustomed to growing up in the LDS church. Even the preacher was hip and youthful, cracking jokes and incorporating little rap numbers into his sermons. I didn't think Christian people could be cool. We kept returning to this surprisingly comfortable, love-filled place for a while until life got in the way again.

My relationship with Dad had taken a turn for the good after Debbie attacked Dad one morning, biting and beating him. Dad called the police, she was taken to jail and Dad began the process of filing for divorce.

Dad had been doing well medically. His heart was strong, and he had been free from his bipolar and schizophrenic tendencies (diagnosed many years earlier). He came to San Diego and spent three days with me, pouring his heart out about the brokenness of his marriage with Debbie. She had been using drugs and physically abusing him for quite a while. As tears welled up in his eyes, I realized I had never seen Dad so vulnerable. It was a sweet time of bonding I rarely experienced with my father.

A few days after Dad returned to Sacramento, he checked himself into a mental hospital because he was suicidal. He had made contact with Debbie, and Debbie convinced him the mental hospital was the best place for him. My siblings told me they were going to get Dad checked out.

It was a few days later that Dad sped into our driveway in his fancy Mercedes in a ferocious rage to belittle Daniel. His threats were serious. The next night, the police banged on our door and served us an eviction notice. We had 30 days to be out of Dad's house, and we owed him $10,000 in back rent.

With no money and no friends, I knew we would be living in a homeless shelter or in our car. I told Dad this, and he didn't care. I confided in my mother-in-law about my father's rage and the events leading up to Dad's explosion that night at our house. Karen, being a pastor's wife, was a very religious woman. She prayed for me that morning and said things like, "God will take care of you. God will work everything out for your good. God will not forsake you."

None of this made sense. *How could any of this be good? We have no money. We have no place to live. Daniel doesn't have a job.*

I couldn't imagine how this situation could work out.

☙☙☙

A cloud of darkness hung over our lives. Our 600-square-foot loft on Fifth and Broadway was in the worst neighborhood in downtown San Diego. The streets below our building proliferated with prostitution, drug dealing and homelessness.

Rose had been diagnosed as a depressed and melancholic child. She reminded me of Eeyore from

Winnie the Pooh. She had trouble in school and didn't participate much in the classroom. But she kept asking to go back to Canvas Church. It gave her a spark, so we began attending regularly.

The people at Canvas showed my family amazing love. Right after Dad evicted us, the pastor's wife, Katie, approached us after the service. She could sense the trauma and hurt in our lives, but Daniel and I let our pride prevent us from opening up to her.

Katie looked deep into my eyes with genuine passion. "Pastor Ben and I care for you very much. Whatever is going on in your life, we will be praying for you." Even though I had just met her, I felt authentic love and care.

When Rose decided she wanted to get baptized, Daniel and I were excited. Rose wanted to show the world she had trusted Jesus as her Savior and asked him to forgive all the wrong things she had done. She wanted to do this by being publicly immersed under the water at church. My mom and Daniel's parents were coming to San Diego for the baptism. Rose wanted me to get baptized with her. I thought about it, but I still couldn't wrap my mind around some of these Christian concepts. I couldn't understand everything, and I needed to figure everything out for myself before I took this step.

I went to a local community college to enroll in a world religion class. I thought this would help me figure out these religious concepts and come to a conclusion on my own. As I walked back to my car, my characteristic intuition kicked in. *No, Marie. You need to just get baptized. Just do it! You will figure everything else out in time.*

On an October morning in 2010, my daughter and I got baptized together. At Canvas Church, in front of my mom, who was very quiet about it, my family and a full congregation, Pastor Ben immersed me under the water. As he brought me up, I could see walls crumbling down around me. I felt all the junk being washed away, left in the water of the baptismal. God was comforting me and asking me to trust him.

Shortly afterward, I lost my job at the boutique. My intuition told me to use my newfound free time to study the Bible. For the next few months, I studied the Bible daily. I listened to sermons online, I blasted and sang along to music that celebrated God — music I used to think was cheesy.

One sunny January morning, in my 12th-floor loft condo, I received a breakthrough — answers for my many questions. I paced around the living room area listening to a sermon online while music played softly in the background. I could hear the outside sounds of brakes squealing, sirens blaring and the cacophony of city life. I felt so desperate. *I have to get out of here. I have to get my kids out of this.*

I had been running my life my way for so long, and my way obviously wasn't working. I could see now that so many times, God had "thrown me overboard," letting my own decisions take me into the deep end of circumstances. He was trying to get my attention, and I kept ignoring him, trying to do things on my own. I had nothing left to do but cry out to God.

My knees buckled from underneath me, and I hit the floor, warm from the sunlight streaming through the window. Sobbing, I threw my hands up and surrendered everything. "God, have your way! I am giving you my all! This time, I am yours. Whatever you want me to do, I will do it, wherever you want me to go, I will go!"

I had read many of the promises God gives in the Bible. When I actually decided to give God control of my life, I could see the truth of those promises coming to fruition in my life. God promises if we follow him, we will have peace, and even in the midst of my turmoil in that noisy downtown apartment, I did have peace. For the first time, I was finally at peace with my life. Peace had been foreign to me, but I no longer worried about every aspect of my life and how all my circumstances would work out. I often looked at our budget and wondered how we would have food on the table or clothes on our backs, but we have never gone without. God has provided for our every need and blessed us with more than we thought possible. I know God is in control, and the plan he has in place is perfect.

After forgiving my dad so many times throughout my life, I knew I must, once again, forgive him for everything he had done to my family. God promises to heal the brokenhearted, and he healed my heart enough to forgive my dad. I fought God over verbalizing this forgiveness to Dad — I had forgiven him so many times, yet his actions never changed. I didn't want to give him a reason to justify his actions. But I knew I couldn't grow closer to God if I didn't let go of my hardness toward him. Besides, how could I withhold from Dad the love and forgiveness Jesus recklessly showed toward me and my many sins? In a brief conversation with Dad the summer after my baptism, God granted me the strength I needed for that important step.

"Dad, I forgive you. I am praying for your marriage with Debbie, and I am praying for our relationship." Those few words, spoken from my heart, released me from the anger and hostility I had harbored against him. It didn't take a psychiatrist, physiologist, self-help books or seminars. It was God and nothing else! Despite my mom hating my dad, despite my siblings hating my dad and despite my own resistance to forgive, God helped me forgive. And I believe, with time, God will help me forget, too.

The dark cloud that hung over my daughter's life for so many years lifted as well. Rose completely transformed from the depressed, melancholic child into an outgoing ray of sunshine. Her school teachers have called to tell me she is a completely different child from when we first moved to San Diego; she isn't sulking around, she has a large group of friends, she interacts in the classroom. They have told me, "Whatever you are doing, keep doing it!" Rose continues to thrive at church, and she loves the Lord.

Six months after surrendering my life to the Lord, the lease on our dark downtown San Diego apartment ran out. We were desperate to get a fresh start in life, but our budget gave little hope of finding a three-bedroom home in a good neighborhood. Our many searches came up empty. After nearly giving up, a beautiful three-bedroom home in a perfect, family-friendly neighborhood popped up on the rental market. And it was $50 under what we had budgeted! We moved as soon as we signed the lease.

Not only did the living Jesus bring me out of the darkness caused by anger, abuse, false spirituality and hurt, but he brought my whole family out of the dark part of San Diego. We were able to get away from the darkness of Fifth and Broadway and move into the light of a safe new home.

"'For I know the plans I have for you,' declares the Lord, 'plans to prosper you and not to harm you, plans to give you a hope and a future. Then you will call on me and come and pray to me, and I will listen to you. You will seek me and find me when you seek me with all your heart'"(Jeremiah 29:11-13).

THE SWEET LIFE
The Story of Joshua
Written by Karen Koczwara

They say every good chef has his secrets. And for years, I had mine.

やややや

I was born on February 28, 1988 in Baton Rouge, Louisiana. I was the youngest of three kids, following a brother five years my senior and a sister two years older. From birth, I struggled with asthma, often landing in the hospital and hooked up to machines when my breathing grew labored.

"Your son has an especially bad case," the doctors told my parents gravely. "He doesn't seem to be responding to medication at all. I suggest you keep him home as much as possible. This is very serious."

When I was 3 months old, my parents moved to Maine, where my father took a job as a youth pastor. In November 1990, some ladies from the church said, "We are praying for your son." From that moment on, I never struggled with asthma again.

We moved to Newport, Pennsylvania, when I was in kindergarten, and my father took another job as a pastor. My parents enrolled me in a private Christian school, hoping to teach me good morals and values. But when I was in fifth grade, my sheltered world was rocked one afternoon.

As I played around on my brother's computer, I came across some dirty photos. *I know he shouldn't be looking at these,* I thought uneasily. I quickly deleted the Web sites and tried to put the images out of my mind.

In November 1998, my father sat our family down for an announcement, his face sober as he cleared his throat. "I've been having an affair with another woman," he confessed. "I am deeply sorry for what I've done."

I sat frozen in my seat, eyes wide as I watched my father, the man I admired, try to hold it together. Our family was quiet; no one knew quite what to say or do. I had never seen anyone so sorry for what he'd done in my entire life. I loved my father, but what would this mean for our family? Would we have to move away? Would we have to leave the church?

"The woman Dad had an affair with is my friend's mother," my sister whispered to me later that afternoon. "What do you think is going to happen to us now?"

I shook my head. "I don't know," I replied nervously. I hoped someone had the answers around here, because I certainly didn't.

My father confessed what he'd done to the church shortly after. My siblings and I stayed home, while my mother went to the service to support him. The tension in our home grew thick. I heard my parents fight behind closed doors at night, my mother's sobs echoing down the hall as I tried to fall asleep. At the dinner table, we stirred our food around on our plates, our clanging forks a welcome sound in an otherwise silent room. My mother's eyes were sad, but she tried to stay strong for our family.

"I just want you all to know I'm stepping down from my position at the church," my father said one day after the big announcement. "I found work as a car salesman, and I'll do that for now while I seek counseling. Your mother and I are not going to get a divorce, so please don't be worried."

I had never seen my father so humble. I admired him for his honesty and was thankful he and my mother were going to try to repair their marriage. Despite my mother's pain and frustration, they fought to work things out. And every day, my mother's eyes regained a little more hope.

In the sixth grade, I decided to take a peek at those photos I'd seen on my brother's computer. One day after school, when no one was around, I clicked on a few Web sites, surprised at how easy it was to find pictures of naked ladies. My heart raced a bit as I stared at the women; I felt as though I'd been inducted into a secret club. In my heart, I knew what I was doing wasn't right, but I couldn't stop staring. And when I went to bed that night, the images popped right back up in my mind.

I started public school that year and was thrust into the "real" world outside my Christian bubble. I soon picked up on swear words and other slang I'd never heard at church. *I'm not a bad kid,* I told myself. *I'm just doing what everyone else here does.*

My father, who'd gone to dental school before

becoming a pastor, found work as a dental technician for a while. Wanting to get involved in the church setting again, he eventually found his way back to a pastor position in 2001. We moved across the state of Pennsylvania, and I started yet another new school. The timing couldn't have been worse, as I was just on the brink of adolescence.

My pornography problem grew worse, and a thrill rose in my chest as I scanned through the naughty Web sites. I looked forward to every opportunity I had to take "just a few peeks" at the computer. I stayed away from magazines, as those were too risky.

I kept my secret tucked away, too ashamed to tell anyone.

☙ ☙ ☙

When high school rolled around, I threw myself into sports, playing everything from basketball, soccer, cross country and track. On the weekends, I attended youth group at our church. We had a new youth pastor who looked as though he couldn't be much older than us. My sister and I often joked about his age.

"He looks like he could still be in high school," she whispered, giggling.

One evening, my mother invited him over for dinner. I immediately liked him; he was funny, friendly and open about his struggles in life. After dinner, I pulled him aside. "Do you think I could talk to you sometime?" I asked. "I'm kinda dealing with something."

"Of course, Joshua," he replied. "Anytime."

The next time we met, I told him about my pornography problem. "I just can't stop looking," I confessed, my head hung in shame. "Every time, I say it's going to be the last, and then I do it again."

He nodded, his eyes warm and understanding. "You know what, Joshua? You're not alone. I used to struggle with pornography just like you, and I eventually confessed it to my peers at church. They kicked me off the leadership and drama team, and I was totally humiliated. I lost the respect of my friends and the people I cared about most. I felt really rotten for a while, but then I found a great group of guys who met with me on a regular basis and prayed for me. I began checking in with them and letting them know if I'd slipped up or not during the week. If I had, they didn't make me feel bad. They simply prayed for me again and reminded me they were here if I needed to talk. That really meant a lot. If you want, I can do the same for you."

I was blown away by his words. "Wow, thanks for being so open," I said gratefully. "That really means a lot to me. I would love it if you prayed for me." I was relieved to know I was not alone. If my youth pastor had struggled and found hope and freedom from his addiction, I could, too.

From that moment on, I had a newfound respect for my youth pastor. We became like brothers, and I could hardly wait to get to church every week to talk to him. I prayed, asking God to help me keep my eyes away from the computer. One afternoon, I slipped up. I immediately felt terrible and decided to tell my father. My youth pastor said the most important thing was to tell someone so they could keep me accountable, and I knew I could trust my father.

"Dad, I messed up today and looked at some stuff on the computer that I shouldn't have," I told him. "I feel really bad about it."

"You know what, son?" My father looked me straight in the eyes. "I know you see yourself as a terrible, disgusting person, but God doesn't see you that way. He sees you as a mighty warrior."

His words meant the world to me. I knew he had struggled with those same feelings of self-loathing when he had his affair, but he had asked God to forgive him and had forgiven himself. If he could find freedom from those feelings, so could I.

"Help me, God, to be strong. I want to be that mighty warrior my dad says I am," I prayed.

That winter, I attended a retreat camp with my youth group. One night, after the youth pastor spoke, he asked those of us who wanted to give our hearts back to God to come forward. I stood and slowly walked to the front of the room. I had invited Jesus into my life as a young boy, but until now, I had not truly committed my whole heart to him. "God, please forgive me of the wrong I've done. I want to give my whole heart to you. Please help me to make *you* the most important thing in my life."

Though I didn't date any girls throughout high school, I found something else I was passionate about: cooking and baking. I took several cooking classes and enjoyed every aspect of them, from the beginning of the project to the final result. My cooking teacher shared with us that she had lost her husband to a brain tumor.

"Cooking became very therapeutic for me," she said. "Working in the kitchen helped me get through this very difficult time."

During study halls, I took the hall pass and escaped to the cooking room to help out. Since I was allergic to shellfish, I decided to stick with baking rather than cooking. The menu items were endless, but I took a special interest in baking bread. I loved the way the soft dough felt in my hands as I kneaded it, loved picking out special spices and flavors and loved the fresh smell as it came out of the oven. It was easy to see why my teacher had found such comfort in baking during tragedy.

My senior year, I decided I might want to go to culinary school. Folks around church began to shake their heads, perplexed that I didn't want to pursue ministry like my father.

"Culinary school? That's a bit ... unusual," one man said. "Are you sure that's what you want to do with your future?"

"I'm positive," I replied confidently.

"Well, I guess you're just the black sheep of the family," he said with a laugh.

But I'd never been so sure of anything in my life. After graduation, I applied to the Culinary Institute of America in Hyde Park, New York, and was accepted into the baking and pastry program. Top chefs had graduated from the school, and I knew the experience could lead to a promising career. New York would be a big stretch for a boy who'd spent his life in church groups. But I grew excited as I packed my things and prepared for adventure. What better way to reach out to others and share God's love with people than in a new setting like this?

Hyde Park, a small town nestled on the Hudson River, was a far cry from the bustling city of skyscrapers and endless nightlife in New York City 90 miles away. With the sprawling green properties and large brick houses, it reminded me of the places I'd grown up. But life at the culinary school was not quite so picture perfect. Drugs, booze and parties ran rampant off campus, and I quickly felt terribly out of place.

"Why did you bring me here to New York?" I questioned God. "I haven't met anyone else who goes to church, and it's getting pretty lonely."

I focused on learning as much as I could during my time at the institute, reminding myself that I was getting some of the best culinary training in the country. I eventually found a Christian group that met at school, and I joined it. But it was difficult to connect with others, and I grew lonelier than ever. How could I be supposedly living my dream and yet be so miserable?

Halfway through the program, I got an externship at the prestigious Hotel Hershey in Hershey, Pennsylvania. Built in the 1930s, Hotel Hershey is known as one of America's landmark hotels. It boasts beautiful green grounds with stunning architecture, miles of fitness trails and quaint cottages that back up to the dense Pennsylvania woods. Again, from the outside, it seemed like the storybook setting, but there, I hit a new low.

The school assigned me to employee housing for the next three months. It seemed exciting at first — a chance to meet new friends, maybe bond over pizza and movies after work and swap culinary stories of the day. But my new roommates were gone all the time, leaving behind a disgusting trail of dirty clothes, empty food containers and booze. One evening, when I went downstairs to watch TV, I saw an arrest report lying on the table. Curious, I picked it up and was disturbed to learn my roommates had been arrested for doing drugs and having drug paraphernalia around the house.

"I've gotta get out of here," I murmured to myself.

I called a friend who lived in the area and asked if I might be able to rent a room from him.

"Of course," he agreed. "I've got space."

I thanked God for my new setting and for my friend's willingness to house me. After I finished the externship, I returned to Hyde Park for the last part of my schooling. The partying, drugs, swear words and booze were everywhere, and I felt horribly out of place again. I thought of my high school days, my youth group and my family back home. Things had seemed so much simpler then. Here, I felt like a foreigner in a strange land. Why had God brought me to New York, anyway?

One night, as I lay in bed reading my Bible, I stumbled onto a passage in the Old Testament book of Ezekiel. The passage told a story of a man who had stumbled into the middle of a valley full of dry bones. God told the man to speak to the bones and tell them that God would breathe life back into them. The man did as he instructed, and as he spoke, the bones came together and flesh appeared on them. But there was still no breath in them. God then told the man that the bones represented the people of Israel, who felt they had no hope. He said that he wanted to settle the people of Israel in their new land, bring new life to them and offer hope that could only come through him.

I read through the passage several times. It seemed like a strange story at first, but the more I pored over it, the more sense it made to me. God had brought me to my own valley of dry bones, a place that seemed dark, lonely and hopeless. But I now saw the purpose in my circumstances; he had brought me to New York to bring life to others. He wanted me to share the good news of his love with those who did not know him. I had spent my entire life in comfortable settings, but I might never return to those places again. It was time to step out of my comfort zone and live for God, no matter where I lived or what I did.

Over the next few weeks, I wrote a series of letters I entitled "The Ezekiel Letters." In them, I poured out my heart to God as I jotted down specifically what I wanted to accomplish while in New York. I would look at this place as an opportunity from him going forward and pray that God would put people into my life who needed to hear about him.

As I completed my time at the institute, I searched for chances to share God's love with others. When one of my friends grew discouraged, I told him what God had done in my life. "None of us are perfect, but he is the only one who can bring hope," I told him. "No matter what you've done, it's never too late to turn your life around for God. The world offers temporary happiness, but real joy isn't found in a beer bottle or at the next party. It's found in trusting in God."

I graduated in 2008 and was excited when an opportunity as a culinary assistant at another school arose. A family from the church I'd started attending offered to rent me a room during my schooling, and I was grateful for their hospitality. I began the program in February 2009, and in November of that year, I met a pretty student named Jessica at school.

"What are you doing for the holidays?" she asked one day.

"I think I'm gonna go down to San Diego. I have family down there. What about you?"

"Small world! I'm actually from San Diego, and I'm heading back there for Christmas myself. We should meet up, and I can show you around. It's a great place ... tons to do."

"That would be great!"

I met up with Jessica that Christmas in San Diego and enjoyed exploring the beaches, the neat restaurants and other tourist attractions with her. The warm climate was a welcome change from the frigid New York winters, and I decided it might not be a bad place to settle down someday.

I quickly fell for Jessica, but I was cautious. I'd only had one girlfriend in my life, and I'd kind of put the idea of dating aside when I started school. But Jessica was different than any girl I'd met in a long time; she was fun, sweet and seemed genuine. I loved that we shared a common interest in baking as well.

"I love those gourmet donuts back in New York," I told her. "I'd love to create different flavorful donuts like those someday."

"Those are the best," Jessica agreed with a laugh. "I think I'm going to stick to cake decorating. That's what I love best."

The more time I spent with Jessica, the more I liked her. I prayed and decided to write her a letter one day. "I really like you, but I'm just wondering how you feel about me. I'm also wondering how you feel about God. I know we haven't talked much about that aspect, but it's a really important part of my life."

Shortly after she got the letter, Jessica texted me with a reply. "I've always believed in God, but I haven't been to church in so long. I'd really like to go back, though. I've really enjoyed the time we've been spending together, and I like you, too."

I was thrilled by her response. We started attending church together, and Jessica gave her full heart over to God.

I got a job at a bakery and proposed to her; she happily

accepted. An opportunity arose for me in Kansas during that time, and after praying, I decided to take it.

"It's just for a short time," I promised her. "Then we'll be together again."

As I packed my things, I prayed, thanking God for the new opportunity. *Once again, you're taking me out of my comfort zone, but I know you have a purpose for this, too.* I thought of those lonely days in Hyde Park, the nights I'd spent wondering what on earth it was all for. I now realized that if I had not come to New York, I would not have met Jessica, and she was the best thing that had ever happened to me.

Jessica and I married on July 16, 2011 and moved to San Diego. Jessica's stepmom had a house near the downtown area, and she agreed to rent it to us for a good price. We decided to open up a business baking breads and other sweets. The dream I'd begun from the minute I baked my first loaf of bread in high school was now becoming a reality, and I could only thank God for allowing it to happen.

One evening while reading my Bible, I flipped to a passage in 2 Corinthians 2:14-16:

> But thanks be to God, who ... uses us to spread the aroma of the knowledge of him everywhere ... an aroma that brings life.

This is my verse, God, I prayed excitedly as I read the verse again. He had sent me to New York to be that "life-giving aroma," to encourage others and grow closer to him during an otherwise dark time. I thought of those who'd been skeptical when they learned I didn't plan to follow in my father's footsteps in ministry. It was true, I wasn't a pastor of a church, but I could use the gifts I'd been given as a baker to please God and reach others. Suddenly, I knew the perfect name for our business.

"Aroma of Life. What do you think?" I ran it by Jessica the next day.

"I love it," she agreed. "It says it all."

"Yes, it does, doesn't it?" I smiled.

As Jessica settled into life in downtown San Diego, she began brainstorming new recipe ideas we could use. I planned to focus on delicious gourmet donuts, like the ones I'd sampled in New York. Though Jessica's specialty was cake decorating, I knew we'd make a perfect pair, not only as husband and wife, but as business partners, too. I thanked God for bringing me a woman who shared my same passion. I was more than just lucky; I was blessed.

Jessica and I checked out various churches in the area, but none quite seemed like the right fit. Then, one Sunday, we walked through the doors of Canvas Church, and we immediately felt at home.

The pastor was honest and genuine as he spoke, and I appreciated his authenticity. As a young boy who'd once tried to hide his shameful secret of pornography addiction, I'd felt alone in my struggle for years. Canvas Church seemed like a place where I could be real, let my guard down and truly be myself. I looked forward to returning and connecting with others.

"Hey, check this out," I said to Jessica on the way out, pointing to a table of bagels and coffee outside. "Maybe next week we could bake something and bring it."

"Great idea," she agreed.

We returned the following week with a plate of hot scones. We were glad to share these goodies with new friends, but I knew the secret to the "sweet life" was more than the sugar and spice of the scones themselves. It was a life with God, the "bread of life," who'd been feeding me from the start.

PERFECTLY EMPTY
The Story of Clarissa
Written by Joy Steiner Moore

For almost a week, I had planned it. The pills were stashed safely at home in the medicine cabinet, waiting for their big moment. The day had finally come for me to end my life.

Now, every remaining minute that I lived seemed tragically epic in some way. My 12 years of life were winding down, hour by hour, and I mentally checked off each event as my last. My last homework assignment. My last bedtime. My last breakfast. My last math class. I sat there in my sixth grade classroom and looked sadly at the boy who sat across the table from me.

I'm never going to see him again, I thought, letting my eyes wander around the classroom to the other kids. *None of them. And they won't see me again. This will be an empty seat tomorrow.*

The thought made me horribly sad, but I didn't know what else to do. I knew for sure that the world would be a better place without me. My eating disorder had created a living hell for my family and for me.

When I was dead, I wouldn't have to live with myself anymore.

That night, after dinner, while my mom cleaned up the kitchen and my dad sat in the living room, I slowly made my way to the bathroom. My time had come. Locking the door behind me, I opened the medicine cabinet and found the bottle of Prozac that my doctor had prescribed for my depression. I held the small bottle in my hands and stared at it, weighing the magnitude of what I was about to do.

My bony fingers shook as they fumbled to open the lid of the bottle and pour out just enough medication to put me out of my misery. I glanced up at my reflection in the mirror. My cheeks were so hollow, I hardly recognized myself anymore. The only thing that looked familiar was the long, dark hair framing my lean face, but recently, even my hair had become thin and coarse. This girl in the mirror was a stranger.

And then, with tears streaming down my cheeks, I took a deep breath and popped the pills into my mouth and swallowed. I cried softly in the bathroom for a little while. Then, heavily, I climbed the narrow stairs to my bedroom, lay across my bed and waited to die.

❧❧❧

Four years earlier, I was a typical 8-year-old little girl with a budding desire to be the *best*. From my grades in school to my extracurricular activities, I was organized, and I worked hard and excelled at almost everything I did. I wanted so much to be perfect. If my parents let me stay up too late, I would put myself to bed. After all, I needed my sleep to keep up my good grades. I created whatever special rules I needed to in order to help me fit into a perfect mold.

PERFECTLY EMPTY

So when my older brother, Roland, had a friend over one hot Texas afternoon, I wanted to play the part of the perfect and impressive little sister by serving them some cold drinks. Serving made me feel important and productive, and it was one of my favorite things to do. Mom was at work, so I was free to poke around the kitchen pantry and see what I could come up with. I was looking for Kool-Aid or lemonade mix or something of that nature. But what I found instead was a large container of chocolate Slim-Fast shake mix.

I wasn't overweight at all. In fact, I was actually perfectly normal and extremely average in size. But something told me if I drank a lot of Slim-Fast, I would get skinnier. If I were skinnier, I would be more beautiful, and I would be well-liked. With those thoughts, I completely forgot what brought me to the pantry in the first place.

Finding a pitcher in the cupboard, I took the entire container of Slim-Fast powder and carefully poured it in. Then I filled the remainder of the pitcher with tap water and stirred until the liquid was smooth and silky brown.

This is going to be amazing! I thought to myself.

I awkwardly tipped the pitcher to pour the mixture into a glass, spilling a little bit on the countertop in the process.

When I took my first sip, it wasn't nearly as good as I had imagined it to be. But if it did the trick, it would be worth it. I took another sip and then another, refilling my glass and drinking, until the pitcher was empty.

"Mom, I don't feel so good," I complained later that

afternoon when she returned home from her job at the bank.

"You don't? I'm sorry, Clarissa. Where does it hurt?"

"My tummy," I moaned.

Secretly, I knew why I was in so much stomach pain. I knew I had overdone it. But I couldn't tell my mom I had used up and drunk all of her Slim-Fast powder. No way. For one thing, my family didn't have enough money lying around to be wasteful. But most of all, I knew she wouldn't approve of me drinking her Slim-Fast. So, with everyone convinced I had a touch of the flu, I was sent to bed to sleep it off.

Unfortunately, this was only the beginning of my self-inflicted abuse. Just as I had been obsessed with being the best in everything else, being skinny suddenly became a new obsession for me. In addition to just being skinny, however, I wanted to be the *best* at being skinny. I needed to be perfect at being perfect.

We were a multicultural, bilingual family (my dad was Colombian, and my mom Caucasian), and for several years extended family lived with us in our home. Sometimes, while my parents worked late, I would eat with my uncle, cousins and brother, so my sudden pickiness about food went overlooked and unnoticed for quite a while. My mom did all of the grocery shopping, and I would go with her, but only so I could read the nutrition labels on the food containers and educate myself concerning calories and fat grams. By the time I was 10, I refused to eat anything that wasn't sugar- or fat-free.

PERFECTLY EMPTY

One day, I was sitting in the school cafeteria, nibbling at the sugar-free pudding I had brought with me for lunch.

"Oh, is that good?" I heard a voice say over my shoulder.

I glanced up to see my beautiful, slender teacher, Mrs. Horn, standing over me.

"Yeah, it is," I answered, dipping my spoon gingerly into the pudding cup.

"I've seen it advertised, and I've been meaning to try it sometime."

"You should. It's really good."

As I watched her walk away, I was elated that Mrs. Horn would even think of listening to *my* pudding recommendation. The teacher's pet in me was thrilled.

She must have noticed that I'm losing weight. And if someone as perfect as Mrs. Horn eats sugar-free pudding, too, I must be doing okay.

At home, I ate cereal and graham crackers for dinner. When my family went out to eat at a restaurant, I ordered grits or soup. I was too scared to eat anything else. I would use mustard as a condiment for everything because, with its lack of calories, it was a safe choice.

As I scrimped more and more in my eating, I also started to withdraw from my friends and family. I had always been very social before, but now I didn't want people to get too close to me and discover what I was doing. I wanted them to admire me from afar and leave it at that.

My parents began to notice the change in both my

eating habits and personality, but they couldn't figure out what was wrong exactly. They made a doctor's appointment for me, and when that one failed to provide answers, they made an appointment with a different doctor.

Over the next few months, we saw a *lot* of doctors. Nobody in the medical field had seen my symptoms and behavior in someone as young as I was, so the doctors hesitated to make a diagnosis.

Desperate, my mom made me an appointment with a holistic doctor who prescribed Aloe Vera juice and recommended that we put a special air filter in the house. My parents complied because they were anxious for *something* to make me better.

Anything was worth a try to bring the life back into the little girl who was becoming more hollow and withdrawn by the day.

Still, nothing worked.

❧❧❧

My feet didn't quite touch the floor, so I swung them nervously beneath the chair where I sat, at the end of the counselor's big brown desk. I looked glumly at my hands, clasped tightly in my lap, while I waited for her to speak.

"This little girl has anorexia," the counselor finally said, quite matter-of-factly.

The words were directed at my mom, but they seemed to echo off the walls of the small office.

What's anorexia?

I felt (more than heard) my mom's big sigh of relief. "Finally!" she exclaimed. "That's what I've thought all along!"

She seemed almost happy about the diagnosis, but I know now that she was simply relieved to have a name for the darkness that was eating away at her 11-year-old daughter ... and to finally have the opportunity to seek treatment for it.

The counselor turned her gaze to me. "Clarissa, you have a disease called *anorexia nervosa.*" Her eyes studied my baggy blue jeans and the way I fidgeted with the sleeve of my oversized shirt. "Anorexia is an eating disorder, but we can help you get better."

A disease? My 11-year-old brain was frightened by that word. "Eating disorder" sounded better to me — like it wasn't set in stone. *Who decides what an eating disorder is, anyway?*

Though I wasn't happy inside, I certainly didn't want to get better, either. I was hooked on this lifestyle, and I no longer knew myself apart from it. Somewhere in this darkness hovering over me, I had completely lost Clarissa. I had become one with the unknown force controlling me. I was exhausted, but I was in too deep now. I knew I couldn't get better, but in the back of my mind, I was toying with an idea I had that would get me out altogether.

So a few months later, on a chilly January evening, when I couldn't take it anymore, I overdosed on pills and laid on the bed, staring at the ceiling and waiting to die. I wanted more than anything to just silently slip away, out of my body, out of this life.

The room grew darker as I lay there, and soon the only light in my room was the light from the hallway peeking through the crack under my door. Outside my window, everything seemed normal. The occasional car passed by my house, and I listened to the lone sound of a motorcycle fade away as it got farther down the street. Our neighbors were taking out their trash. An airplane flew overhead. Life would go on without me.

Already, nausea and weakness were starting to set in.

Downstairs, the TV was on, and through my locked bedroom door, I could hear the muffled laugh-track of the sitcom my dad was watching. My mom was moving around the kitchen, and dishes were clattering lightly in the sink. They didn't know that their daughter was upstairs dying — that tonight they would discover her lifeless body and have to begin the grim task of making funeral arrangements.

My brother Roland was in the bedroom next to mine, dutifully completing his homework. I wouldn't be turning my homework in tomorrow; in fact, I hadn't even bothered to do it. Hayley, my baby sister, was already asleep in her crib for the night. I thought about her sweetness and what joy she had brought to my family in the midst of the turmoil I had caused. It pained my heart that she would grow up without me.

Suddenly, I couldn't take it. I was overcome with guilt,

and I wasn't sure that I really wanted to die after all. Well, yes, I wanted to die. But as much as I hated myself, I loved my family, and I didn't *really* want to hurt them. I was scared that I had made a big mistake.

What if it's too late?

I unlocked the door and stumbled down the stairs.

"Mom?"

"Yes, sweetheart?"

"Um, I just took a bunch of pills, and um …"

"What do you mean? How many did you take?" Her face showed her panic.

"A lot."

"Why? Were you trying to hurt yourself?" She grabbed the cordless phone.

"Yes."

"Oh, my gosh! Alvaro, come here!"

She quickly dialed 911 as my father ran into the room. The next few minutes were a blur for me as an ambulance arrived, and I was swiftly loaded onto a stretcher and sped to the hospital, sirens blaring. My stomach was pumped, and a tube the size of a garden hose was shoved down my throat. The doctors gave me activated charcoal, which absorbs and binds toxic drugs. It was a close call, but they saved my life.

For days after I was released from the hospital, I vomited charcoal all over our house. It was extremely unpleasant for everyone. More than anything, though, my parents were distraught over my psychological wellbeing. More than once I heard my mom say, "What are we going to do with her?" Very suddenly my situation had become life threatening. The eating disorder wasn't a cute condition; it had morphed into self-destruction on multiple levels. I was a complete mess.

In fact, despite their best efforts, over the next three years, I would attempt suicide seven more times.

 తతత

The following August, I was admitted to Children's Hospital. I was so sick by this point that the specialists gave me a 50 percent chance of survival. They told my parents there was only so much they could do. They gave me disposable feeding tubes and made me drink Scandishakes, which were 3,000-calorie drinks that provided nutrition and caused weight gain. Eventually, I was healthy enough to go home, but I definitely wasn't cured. I refused to eat what my mom cooked, and within a few weeks, I was down to 58 pounds.

My parents had heard of an expensive treatment center in Wickenburg, Arizona, called Remuda Ranch. It wasn't just expensive; at $3,000 per day, it was out of the question. But my parents felt like it was my best shot, so my mom made a bunch of fliers telling of my situation and our financial need, and she distributed them everywhere she could. They had to have a $10,000 down payment just to get me started. Amazingly, through the generosity of several local churches in our city of Arlington, they pulled enough money together.

PERFECTLY EMPTY

At 12 years old, I was the youngest person ever admitted to Remuda Ranch. My mom and dad flew with me to Arizona. When we arrived, I was struck by the beauty of the campus and its Southwestern charm. Adorable white stucco buildings with red villa-style roofs were surrounded by palm trees and long paths that wound through the lovely grounds. There were horses for riding and even a swimming pool. My dad filmed our arrival with his video camera. Small and feeble, I was immediately assigned a wheelchair and given a permanent feeding tube. My parents stayed a few days, and once I was settled, they left me there.

Remuda Ranch proved to be an amazing place for me. The treatment center was church-affiliated, so the counseling was intense, and we sang religious songs. I made a lot of friends, and as my health improved, I rode horses almost every day. On my 13th birthday, one of my new friends gave me a giant teddy bear that was nearly as big as I was. I really wanted to get better, but not enough to truly recover. In the three months I stayed at Remuda Ranch, I went from a sickly 58 pounds to a much more manageable 91.

As my time in the program neared its end, I began to dread going home to Texas. I didn't trust my parents; they just wanted me to be fat. I also didn't relish the fact that I would have to go and join my classmates in the middle of seventh grade. I wished I could stay at the heavenly ranch forever, but I didn't have a choice.

At home, though supposedly better, I was miserable. I

tried to continue my recovery, but I felt like I was back where I started. I immediately slipped into old habits, obsessively restricting my diet and ultimately terrified of food. My poor parents must have wanted to give up on me. Here they had just gone into debt nearly $300,000 for my treatment, and though I had gained weight, my mindset had not changed a bit. Even so, they wouldn't stop fighting for me.

They put me on a plane to Arizona, this time to a different treatment center in the city of Chandler. Every time I went to a new hospital, I compared myself to the other anorexic girls around me.

I'm better at restricting than she is, I would think to myself. *I have more bones showing.*

I wanted to be the best at being skinny, and sadly, my relationships with the other Type A perfectionist girls in the treatment centers were only adding fuel to the fire.

Regardless of the fact that I had learned a few of the friends I had made at Remuda Ranch had already passed away, I still hadn't found my own reason to survive.

The next two years were a rollercoaster of emotions as I continued my old habits of restricting food and attempting suicide. I stayed at a total of 14 different hospitals and treatment centers, in Arizona, Texas and Oklahoma. Since I would be in class for a few days, then get worse and have to go to another hospital, I had missed several years of school. When I was almost 14, my parents believed I was stable enough to start going to school full-time again.

"Clarissa, what do you think about attending a boarding school in Colombia?" my dad asked one day. He always spoke to us in his native Spanish so that we would become fluent. "There's an all-girl sister school to the private school that I attended as a boy. It would be fun for you, and you would be exposed to my culture."

"*Sí*, I would like that!"

I had always liked adventure, and I looked forward to getting to know my grandmother and extended family better, so I jumped at the chance.

I moved to Colombia, South America, just in time to start my eighth grade year. The boarding school was extremely elite, and the class work difficult. As the only American and only English-speaking student at the school, I was forced to speak in Spanish all the time. During the weeknights, I shared a large room with 11 other girls on the campus, but on the weekends, I was allowed to travel to my grandmother's village and spend time with my aunts, uncles and cousins. It was comforting to be near family, but even with the new start and the different cultural experience, I was still haunted by my old demons.

One night early in the second semester, I lay in the dark, struggling with my old thoughts of worthlessness. There was a darkness hovering over me that I couldn't seem to shake. Hopelessness and oppression had followed me, and again, tragically, I knew there was only one way out. I dared myself to go through with it.

There were 12 twin beds in the room, half on one wall and half on the other, with a walkway in the middle. As I lay in my bed, I listened to the rhythm of my roommates' breathing and determined when they were all finally asleep. I reached for my bottle of antidepressant pills in the drawer of my nightstand and quietly popped the lid open. My body trembled as I poured about half the bottle into my waiting open hand, then two pills at a time, put them in my mouth and swallowed. It was done. I lay back down and waited. It would only be a matter of time now.

Within minutes, I began to feel sick to my stomach. I thought I might vomit. I hated throwing up. In all the years I had had an eating disorder, I had never ever been good at being bulimic. I might die here now, but I certainly didn't want to vomit all over myself. I was already getting weak, so I rolled out of bed and began to crawl slowly across the long room to the bathroom we all shared.

"Clarissa is so sweet!" a voice behind me said in English.

"I know! She is going to do so much for the world. I wish she knew how special she is," a second American voice answered.

I turned slightly and saw two girls I had never seen before sitting on a bed talking. One girl had beautiful dark skin with black hair wound in dozens of tightly-woven braids. The other girl had long shiny reddish hair cascading down her back. They were wearing clean white pajamas, unlike anything my roommates wore.

Who are they?

"Yes. She keeps trying to hurt herself, and I just don't understand why," the first girl said, shaking her head. "She's so beautiful."

My heart felt sick with guilt. *What am I doing?* I didn't know who those girls were or what they were doing there, but I had to get the pills out of my system. I crawled faster, using all the strength I could find in my beat-up body to make it to the bathroom. I crawled to the toilet and immediately began sticking a finger down my throat, trying to gag myself.

After several attempts, I was successful, but the pills had already started taking effect. The world seemed fuzzy. I closed my eyes and held on tight to both sides of the toilet seat. I breathed deeply and tried to regain my balance.

I want to live. I want to live. I want to live.

But my body hit the cold tile floor, and darkness enveloped me.

ॐॐॐ

Hours later, I woke up in a hospital bed, nurses buzzing around me. My grandmother and aunt were crying softly in a corner of my room.

"Abuela?" My mouth was dry, and my throat sore. It hurt to speak.

My grandmother rushed to my side. "Oh, Clarissa! What have you done?" she cried in Spanish.

I realized that although this was considered normal behavior for me, and my parents had become used to the suicide drama, this was all very new and shocking to my South American family. Of course, they were all well aware of what I had been through in the previous years, but they had never experienced it firsthand. I felt guilty for causing them such stress.

"I'm so sorry," I managed.

My grandmother kissed me then, and my aunt crossed the room to hold my hand.

"You're going to be okay," my aunt explained. "You passed out on the bathroom floor, but someone found you in time."

"I want to live," I said simply. And for the first time, I truly meant it. My mind flashed back to those two girls that I had overheard talking about me. I knew they didn't belong at the school. I was the only English-speaking student enrolled there. It made no sense that two obviously American girls would have been sitting in our room in the middle of the night.

Did I dream it? No, I knew it was real. It had been so vivid to me. I could still see them clearly in my mind's eye.

Their clothing had been so pure, so ... *otherworldly.* It was almost as if they didn't belong on earth. And the things they had said: "She is going to do so much for the world ... how special she is." Did they really believe that? Did I truly have it in me to be anything other than damaged goods? And why did they care? It made no sense to me.

I knew one thing. I was sick of being sick. I wanted to go home to the States and get better for good. And whoever those girls were, they made me never want to kill myself again. Their words, as simple as they were, had intervened in my self-destruction, launching me out of my darkness and into the light.

I want to live.

꙰꙰꙰

After I flew home to Texas, my family sent me to one last hospital in nearby Dallas to finish my mental healing process. It was actually a good experience for once. I had a good doctor, and I was on the road to full recovery.

The incident with the mysterious girls that last night at the boarding school kept replaying through my mind, and I began to believe that maybe God had had something to do with it.

When I was a little girl, my family had attended a church regularly. I had learned about God's son, Jesus, in Sunday school and how he had come to earth to take my punishment for all the things I had done wrong. I had loved Jesus, and every night when I said my prayers, I asked him to always hold my hand. But as I gradually became obsessed with being perfect — downing Slim-Fast, learning to count calories and scrimping during meals — I gradually let go of Jesus' hand. I was trying to become perfect all on my own. Now I felt very alone and distant from him.

Since I was in the hospital, I had plenty of time to sit and think. I hadn't really thought about God for a long time, but slowly, it all started coming back to me.

Those girls weren't human. God sent them to stop me.

What else could explain it?

God must want me to live.

I should have been dead, eight times over. Yet, here I was, getting better and *wanting* to live for the first time in years. There was no logical explanation for the drastic shift in my thinking — for the light switch being turned on so suddenly.

Somewhere in the back of my mind, I remembered something I had learned as a little girl. It was found in the Bible: "'For I know the plans I have for you,' declares the Lord. 'Plans to prosper you and not to harm you, plans to give you hope and a future'" (Jeremiah 29:11).

God has plans for me, I thought. *He doesn't want me dead.* If God had gone out of his way to wake me up, certainly I could take his hand! Wouldn't it be nice to feel as safe and secure as I used to?

God, thank you for saving me! my heart cried. *Jesus, please hold my hand again!*

Peace instantly filled me. The darkness lifted, and I felt calm for the first time in years. I was God's child again, and the best part was, I no longer felt like I needed to be more perfect. I was enough, just as I was. I didn't know what to call it then, but I was experiencing God's grace.

PERFECTLY EMPTY

సౌసౌసౌ

When I was healthy, both physically and mentally, the doctor released me to go home. It felt so good to be *normal* again. I was no longer afraid of food, and I was no longer afraid of myself. More than ever, though, I was aware of the pain I had put my family through. It was as if I finally woke up and realized I wasn't the only person in the world. I had been asleep to everyone else's problems for so long. But I was done with all that.

Life at home was very different than it had been. The old Clarissa had returned, but financially, my family's life was in ruins. When I was 15, my dad lost his job, and my parents went bankrupt because of all the millions of dollars in medical bills they had accrued for my treatment. I knew it was my fault, and I felt extremely guilty about it.

On Saturday mornings, my mom, Hayley and I would drive our beat-up car down to the Arlington Charity to get our food for the week. The people at the charity were so nice, but it was very humbling for us to accept help.

"We might be on the streets soon," Mom confided in me on one of those Saturday morning pick-ups. "I think we're going to lose the house."

My heart sank.

"Where will we go?"

"Um, a shelter?" Mom shrugged, and I took that to mean that was her best guess.

I was worried. I decided to turn to my newfound faith. If God could wake me up, certainly he could keep us out of a shelter, too. So I began to plead with him to help my family.

We had an old Bible on our bookshelf, so I found it and took it down. I read:

> Look at the birds of the air; they do not sow or reap or store away in barns, and yet your heavenly Father feeds them. Are you not much more valuable than they?
>
> *-Matthew 6:26*

How I loved that! I leaned heavily on those words in the next few weeks as we learned for certain that we would be losing our house. But instead of a shelter, my parents found an apartment they could afford in a nasty apartment complex. It was very small; the entire apartment could have fit in our previous home's living room and kitchen. But it was a place to live, and we were grateful.

More points for God, I silently noted.

School was starting, and I should have been entering my sophomore year in high school, but because I had missed so much over the years, the school system wanted to put me back in sixth grade. My mom went to battle with the school board over it, arguing that I needed to be in a normal place to continue my recovery. Thanks to her, they allowed me to test out of sixth, seventh, eighth and ninth grades.

Since we were living in a new neighborhood, I started 10th grade in a public high school where nobody knew what I had been through. I just wanted to fit in and be normal, but I wasn't sure if I knew how to be social anymore. I had just returned from living in hospitals and treatment centers and then a boarding school in a foreign country, so it was difficult to relate to average school kids who had been leading normal lives. Even so, always the overachiever, I did well in my schoolwork and got really involved in theater and choir. I also picked up several jobs on the side to stay busy and got involved at a local church youth group. I believed that if I stood still, the eating disorder would take over again.

I began to make new friends. Shannon, one of my closer girlfriends, was a ballerina. She was very talented and had been accepted to a summer ballet camp at the Boston Ballet Company. But as our friendship progressed, I spotted the familiar signs of an eating disorder. She picked at her food during lunch, moving it around on her plate with her fork so nobody would notice she wasn't really eating. She was rail-thin and gaunt, so much so that she looked sickly ... like I had been.

One spring afternoon, I invited her to take a walk with me to the park across the street from our high school. We sat down on the green grass and breathed in the fragrance of the blooming azaleas nearby.

"Shannon ..." I began, not really sure how to go about it. I squirmed a bit and played with a dandelion stem by my foot as I searched for the most delicate of words.

Shannon met my gaze, her blue eyes seeming tired and sad. She hugged her scrawny knees to her chest.

"I think you might have an eating disorder," I said.

"No, I don't." She tensed up and stared at me.

"Listen. I know about this stuff. I was anorexic for several years, so I recognize it when I see it."

Shannon hugged her knees tighter and looked at the ground.

"Okay. So?"

"Well, so, you're killing yourself," I answered bluntly. "I can tell you my whole story if you want me to prove it to you, but I know what you're doing. And you know what?"

I paused while Shannon looked me in the eyes.

"You can get better. God helped me get out, and he can help you, too. I can't explain it, but I know it's possible."

An hour passed, and still we sat in the sun, me telling Shannon my story and how I now knew there was light on the other side of the darkness. There was a peace I felt in my life that couldn't be explained. I told her about Jesus, who I believed was sent to earth from heaven to pay the price for all I had done wrong, then take it *all* away from me. I wasn't perfect, and I never would be. But I was a child of God, and thanks to his enormous love, I was sitting there right then *alive.*

"You have two choices," I finally said. "You can let me take you to a hospital right now, or you can go home and tell your parents. But if you don't tell your parents, I will."

Shannon was quiet for a few moments. When she spoke, she admitted that as a ballerina, the pressure to be skinny was enormous. She began to cry softly, and I did, too. I remembered that pressure, and I remembered the darkness that had stalked me for so long. I cried with thankfulness that I had been rescued — that God had saved me — and with hope for her.

That evening, Shannon told her parents about her eating disorder. They took her to the emergency room, and when the nurses checked her vitals, they found that her heart rate was in the 20s. She was already very close to death.

"You got here just in time," the doctor told her parents.

❧❧❧

I graduated from high school with honors, and I headed to the University of North Texas. I thrived in an academic environment and immediately got involved as a peer advisor and resident assistant, helping other girls deal with eating disorders, mental issues, etc. It felt good to be helping other girls. I kept my own former struggles a secret, however, especially since I was working so hard to attain perfection. I began doing it all on my own again, instead of staying close to God. As a result, I began eating less and less. I lost weight, and soon my 5-foot, 8-inch frame was down to 110 pounds.

When I was 20, my mom took me to the doctor, and I was diagnosed with osteopenia, which is pre-osteoporosis. My bones were losing the battle.

I began to realize that the eating disorder would never completely go away; those demons would always be trying to wiggle their way in. But as long as I let God stay in my life, we could keep them out together. It was not something I could do on my own. I began reading the Bible again and focusing my attention on others instead of myself. I read this passage in 1 Corinthians 6:19-20:

> Don't you know that your body is the temple of the Holy Spirit, who lives in you and was given to you by God? You do not belong to yourself, for God bought you with a high price. So you must honor God with your body.

I genuinely loved the thought that my body was considered a "church" for God's Holy Spirit. My body was God's house, not my own. I wanted him to use me to give others that same peace he had brought me. I was here to tell others how Christ saved me, even when the doctors and everyone else (including myself) had given up. I had not deserved to live, yet he miraculously loved me that much.

With a renewed change in focus, I gained weight, and I got better. It was much easier this time around because I already had the answer — I just had to receive it. Even the osteopenia faded away with time as my bones were built back up through an improved diet.

During my senior year of college, the idea of becoming an Army Intern intrigued me — travel and adventure! After graduation, I interviewed in Washington, D.C., and landed a job as a logistician. Over the next four years, I moved to nine states and visited six countries. It was a busy career with a hectic schedule, but I loved every second of it.

In the midst of it all, however, I felt like I wanted to do more for my country. There was a deep yearning in my heart to actually serve. My job felt cushy, and that didn't seem right to me, with so many people risking their lives overseas. So without anyone knowing, I applied for a Presidential Direct Commission to the U.S. Navy. I was shocked a few months later when I actually received it. I was one of the youngest ever to be given that honor.

❧❧❧

Before long, I found myself on a gun range in California on a hot July day, in preparation for an impending deployment to Afghanistan. As I sat in a classroom waiting for the training to begin, I let my eyes scan the faces of the other servicemen. One guy in particular stood out to me. He sat in the back, reading a book and leaning his chair on its back legs.

Wow. That guy is quite possibly the best-looking guy I've ever seen.

Of course, I wasn't interested in starting a relationship. I'd be deploying to Afghanistan soon, and I had a job to do. But that didn't mean we couldn't be friends. His odd combination of confidence, gentleness and bookishness attracted me, and I wanted to meet him. After class, I found a seat next to him on the bus.

"Hi, I'm Clarissa." I extended my hand.

"Liam." He took my hand and smiled warmly. He was as perfect up close as he had looked from across the room. His eyes were a beautiful deep blue.

We talked on the bus that day, and as it turned out, Liam shared my faith in God. He was being deployed to Afghanistan as well, and I looked forward to developing a friendship with him.

Serving in Afghanistan was life changing, like no experience I had ever had before. One of the most rewarding of my responsibilities was serving as the Salvation Army routing point. If people back in the States sent donations (old clothes, toys, etc.) to the local Afghani people, they would come to me first; and since I wasn't allowed to leave the grounds, I worked with a local contractor to distribute the items to Afghani children in orphanages. Even though my other responsibilities were demanding and stressful, I looked forward to this small part of my duties and to receiving the pictures that the contractor would take of the grateful children receiving the goods.

A group of us were driving along an airfield one day when we came across dozens of little Afghani children crying out to us all along the chain-link fence. They were asking for food and water. I looked at each one as we drove past, little dark heads with sweet tan faces, and my heart broke for the helplessness in their eyes. I thought of my 11-year-old self, deep in depression and obsessed with depriving myself of what I needed to grow and be healthy. And yet, it had all been right there — as much food and water as I could have possibly wanted or needed. These children lived the opposite reality. They dreamed of a day when they wouldn't be hungry or thirsty.

"Stop the car!" I shouted to the driver.

Before the Jeep had even rolled to a halt, I was out the door with my bottle of water, heading for the chain-link fence.

Surely I can do this much.

But the Afghani guard at the fence stopped me.

"Don't you know that these children could have bombs? They might be trying to lure you! You cannot get too close."

Tears filled my eyes. I knew he was right.

But these children! They deserve food and drink. How I want them to know God's love!

Sadly, I climbed back into the Jeep, and we drove away. I couldn't help the children then, but I could pray for them. I believed in my heart that God would take care of these children, just like he took care of me.

I attended a church on the base in Afghanistan, and it was exactly what I needed. I finally felt like I was able to do what I had wanted to for years — begin to forgive myself for *everything.* Even though I had been better for quite a while and was able to get through the daily temptations with God's help, I still struggled with guilt over hurting myself and my family for years on end. But with the support and prayers of a little church of service members, I accepted God's forgiveness. And *I forgave myself.* I was free.

There, in a desolate, dark part of the Middle East, I realized that the light in my spirit was bright. The difference in me had become like night versus day. I read in my well-worn Bible: "The light shines in the darkness, and the darkness has not overcome it" (John 1:5).

☙ ☙ ☙

My friend Liam attended the little church with me and held my hand tightly during the times of prayer. We had become quite close during our deployment — even more than just friends. We were also running partners on the base and ran in several races together. A stronger and faster athlete than me, Liam always slowed his pace to match mine, an act I found extremely sweet. I confided in him about my past struggles with anorexia, and with all the pressures that come with living on a military base in the middle of a war, he took special care to make sure I ate enough and stayed healthy. I felt completely undeserving of Liam's love, but with the newfound forgiveness I was feeling from myself and from God, I also believed God was telling me, "This is me, redeeming all those years you spent torturing yourself. This is me, giving you happiness to make up for all the darkness. This is me, making it right."

God did indeed make everything right. After six months in Afghanistan, we returned to the States. Liam gave up a position he was offered in Hawaii to move where I was, in San Diego.

Away from the stress of war, he dated me properly, and in May of 2011, we were married.

"What are you thinking about, Clarissa?" Liam asked one early summer morning while we were finishing up our 5 a.m. run.

Usually we talked and laughed during our runs; sometimes we even prayed. But this morning, we had been quiet so far, content to be lost in our individual thoughts. The steady *thump-thump* of our running shoes hit the pavement in unison. I breathed deeply of the sweet California air, and in the darkness, I smiled to myself.

"How lucky I am. How good God is to me."

We passed under a streetlamp, and in the dim light, I saw a slight smile play on his lips.

"How so?" he asked.

"It just hits me from time to time, how lucky I am to be alive. Even this …" I motioned with my hand to indicate our moving feet. "There was a time when I wasn't healthy enough to run. I was so sick, I was in a wheelchair."

We were silent for a few moments. In the distance, the eastern horizon was showing the first signs of morning light. Other than the chirping of a few lone crickets, the world still seemed very much asleep.

Finally, Liam spoke.

"I'm glad God saved you, too. I feel like *I'm* the lucky one."

I blushed, and I was thankful he couldn't see.

God, thank you for Liam!

We rounded the corner, and I could see our home up ahead — our peaceful, *happy* home. We had left the living room light on, and we ran steadily toward it.

A car passed by us on the street, and we waved to the driver. The sound of a motorcycle faded into the distance. Our neighbor noisily dragged her trashcan down her driveway, and we greeted her with a cheerful "good morning." An airplane flew overhead.

I smiled. "So, what's for breakfast?"

CONCLUSION

My heart is full. When I became a pastor, my desire was to serve as an access point for people to discover Jesus Christ and to see their lives completely changed. My hope was to see hurting people encouraged and filled with hope. This is happening every day at Canvas, as you and I read in these stories. However, rather than being content with our past victories, at Canvas we are spurred to believe that many more can occur.

Every time we see another life beautifully wrecked by an unexpected collision, it increases our awareness that God really loves people, and he is actively seeking to change lives. Think about it: How did you get this book? We believe you read this book because God brought it to you seeking to reveal his love to you. Whether you're a man or a woman, an artist or in the armed forces, blue collar or no collar, a parent or a student, we believe God came to save you. He came to save us. He came to save all of us from the chaos and wreckage we've wallowed in and offer real joy and the opportunity to share in real life that will last forever through faith in Jesus Christ.

Do you have honest questions that such radical change is possible? It seems too good to be true, doesn't it? Each of us at Canvas warmly invites you to come and check out our church family.

Freely ask questions, examine our statements, see if we're "for real" and, if you choose, journey with us at whatever pace you are comfortable. You will find that we are far from perfect. Our scars and sometimes open wounds are still healing, but we just want you to know God is still completing the process of authentic life change in us. We still make mistakes in our journey, like everyone will. Therefore, we acknowledge our continued need for each other's forgiveness and support. We need the love of God now just as much as we did the day before we believed in him.

San Diego's unfolding story of God's love is still being written, and we believe you are a part of it. At Canvas, we realize that everyone has a story, and yours is welcome here. I know as you come with all your troubles and the chaos that surrounds your life you will have an unexpected collision with God's grace, and your life will be beautifully wrecked by his love rather than tragically wrecked by your circumstances.

I hope to see you this Sunday!

Ben Brinkman
Pastor, Canvas Church
San Diego, California

If you are unable to be with us, yet you intuitively sense you would really like to experience such a life change, here are some basic thoughts to consider. If you choose, at the end of this conclusion, you can pray the suggested prayer. If your prayer genuinely comes from your heart, you will experience the beginning stages of authentic life change, similar to those you have read about.

How does this change occur?

Recognize that what you're doing isn't working. Accept the fact that Jesus desires to forgive you for your bad decisions and selfish motives. Realize that without this forgiveness, you will continue a life separated from God and his amazing love. In the Bible, the book of Romans, chapter 6, verse 23 reads, "The result of sin (seeking our way rather than God's way) is death, but the gift that God freely gives is everlasting life found in Jesus Christ."

Believe in your heart that God passionately loves you and wants to give you a new heart. Ezekiel 11:19 reads, "I will give them singleness of heart and put a new spirit within them. I will take away their stony, stubborn heart and give them a tender, responsive heart" (NLT).

Believe that "if you confess with your mouth that Jesus is Lord and believe in your heart that God raised him from the dead, you will be saved" (Romans 10:9 NLT).

Believe in your heart that because Jesus paid for your failure and wrong motives, and because you asked him to forgive you, he has filled your new heart with his life in such a way that he transforms you from the inside out. Second Corinthians 5:17 reads, "When anyone is in Christ, it is a whole new world. [a] The old things are gone; suddenly, everything is new!" (ERV).

Why not pray now?

Lord Jesus, if I've learned one thing in my journey, it's that you are God and I am not. My choices have not resulted in the happiness I hoped they would bring. Not only have I experienced pain, I've also caused it. I know I am separated from you, but I want that to change. I ask you to forgive me for the choices I've made that have hurt myself, others and denied you. I believe your death paid for my sins, and you are now alive to change me from the inside out. Would you please do that now? I ask you to come and live in me so that I can sense you are here with me. Thank you for hearing and changing me. Now please help me know when you are talking to me, so I can cooperate with your efforts to change me. Amen.

If you prayed this prayer and would like to talk to someone, please contact us at 619-231-7745, or you can email us at info@canvasSD.com.

We would love for you to join us at Canvas Church!

Contact Information

Web site: www.canvasSD.com
Email: info@canvasSD.com

Please check out our Web site
for Sunday service times.

Telephone: 619.231.7745

Mailing Address:
10601-G388 Tierrasanta Blvd.
San Diego, CA 92124

Office Hours:
Monday-Thursday, 8:30 a.m. to 4:30 p.m.

For more information on reaching your city with
stories from your church, please contact
Good Catch Publishing at
www.goodcatchpublishing.com

GOOD CATCH
PUBLISHING

Did one of these stories touch you?
Did one of these real people move you to tears?
Tell us (and them) about it on our reader blog at
www.goodcatchpublishing.blogspot.com.